The Right to Life

THE RIGHT TO LIFE

by

A. Delafield Smith

Chapel Hill

THE UNIVERSITY OF NORTH CAROLINA PRESS

To

*Those Esteemed Members
of the Social Work Profession
By Whose Counsel I Have So Greatly Profited
and Whose Abiding Faith in Their Fellow Man
Exemplifies My Philosophy*

Foreword

THE ETHICAL PRINCIPLES upon which the individual nowadays properly founds his claim upon the resources of his society have not, I think, been adequately stated. At any rate, the amount of public controversy that surrounds our present-day social programming bespeaks the grave misgivings with which society views the individual's growing "dependency" upon it.

For one thing, our traditional beliefs concerning the kind and extent of responsibilities that ought properly to be borne by the individual himself in our society have brought to grief many well-conceived attempts to bring about proper adjustments in our modern way of life. Indeed, failure to perceive the sound, ethical bases on which these programs properly rest denies them popular support, gives credence to self-seeking criticism, and even forces the adoption of undesirable statutory patterns.

But this is by no means the worst of the matter—for at the end of our course stands the individual himself. These efforts are in his behalf. And if the true ethical bases of his claims are not recognized either by himself or by his society we must surely fail. Indeed, if in seeking to convince one individual that the security he acquires is rightfully his in token of some highly respected rule of law and justice, we do but teach another that he can never hope to be anything but the pitiful object, or should we say victim, of a despised charity—then indeed, are all our efforts futile. "For what is a man profited if he shall gain the whole world and lose his own soul?"

In our search for the truth, however, we may find ourselves at swords points with widely espoused and treasured points of view. He who would take issue with a popular legend is likely, is he not, to find all society conspiring to defeat him. Perhaps, for example, you have seen or read Alexander Milne's delightful little play called "The Ivory Door." The door itself, you may remember, was located in the throne room. According to the legend, whosoever went through this *ivory door* never came back. He just never came back. You might try it and see for yourself. The youthful King Perivale tried it on his wedding day, quite against the advice of his most sage counselors, and he never came back. However, it occurs to me that his cousin who thereupon succeeded in gaining his throne may have so closely resembled the young king that were it not known that the latter had gone through the ivory door the "distinction" would never have been noticed. So the play ends, but the legend goes on.

The lesson of the play is so clear and the moral so apt as to cause one to question whether it is ever possible to make direct assault upon a highly palatable tradition with any hope of success. This, nevertheless, is just what I seek to do. I feel that we must act upon fundamentally sound ethical premises in order to intelligently improve our social and economic life, and, above all, to strength the morale of the individual and to preserve his spirit.

And so, in the effort to make some headway in so bold a venture, I have sought to call to mind some basic facts and fundamental truths which I believe to be sound and comparatively irrefutable. I would present them, however, against the backdrop of the law and in the light of some of its ancient precepts.

Here, then, is no plea for economic equality, or for placing limits upon the lawful goals of any individual. I do not inveigh against functions privately undertaken for the purposes of upbuilding human capacities or insuring the individual's economic security. The principle of minimum guarantees is, I believe, sound gospel. We are concerned, rather, with the uplifting of society at its base and concerned, too, lest it be found to have weakened at its core. We are concerned, indeed, with the spirit of the individual in our society.

A. Delafield Smith

Washington, D. C.
May 6, 1955.

Contents

The Right to Life

Chapter 1

Legal Highways in Social Science

I took down recently a large octavo volume which, in the effort to be broadly inclusive of all writings on matters of social science over a limited period, restricted itself to brief descriptions of each significant work. I turned to the index but found there no reference whatsoever to law, to legal science, or to legal philosophy. Now it may be that law or jurisprudence was too broad a subject for this social science compendium. But the fact remains that the relation of law in its broadest sense to all those various branches of social science is still for all practical purposes an unexploited, unexplored, and virgin field. Fairly extensive reading and conversation with many authorities confirm this impression. Such subjects as psychology and psychiatry and many other sociological disciplines are being constructed and developed without, as yet, any mature elucidation of the ultimate significance of law and a legally ruled environment to our understanding of human behavior and human reactions. This may be too broad a statement but many will agree that the comment is in general warranted. A good deal of sociological literature seems to concern itself with the legal terrain only to the extent that it may succeed in deprecating, in the light of modern research, many legal methods without realizing what their purpose was. No doubt law is laggard and much of what passes for law is neither sound nor is it law. But the significance of living in a legally ruled environment as a means of promoting individuality, security, and freedom seems to have but a minor influence on the construction of modern social science.

Our society is our own creation. It is man-made, and fundamentally its construction is a law-making process, despite the extent to which one can trace legal rules and principles to pre-existing social conventions. Even so, the processes whereby the conventions were integrated into an effective legal system, the development of legal precedent, and the creation of statutory law were the work of law-conscious minds who were aware of man's basic need of a legally and hence of an ethically ruled environment. Apparently the present great twentieth-century drive is seeking to improve society without adequate recourse to law as a basic science and without adequate knowledge of the real functions of legal methods that seem to those engaged in the drive both archaic and ineffective. No doubt many of them are, but their aims need recognition and achievement. Social science will grossly fail in the long run if it does not build upon the lessons of man's long struggle to preserve and develop the significance of the individual in our society by making him the focal point in a system of legal relationships.

Can we improve what is essentially a legal complex by other than sound legal principles? No one questions the need of sound legal reforms or even some very fundamental transformations of legal concepts. But what eventuates must still be law. Our ultimate aim must be to produce a better legal environment, an environment more conducive to the growth of individuality. This is nominally the central theme of social reform. It is also the goal that made the human race seek a legally ruled society in the first place.

Is it not true that we are devotees of the god of administration today? We are thinking almost wholly in terms of operations and services and of efficiency in method and procedure. We have to remind ourselves from time to time that we cannot rehabilitate individuals any more than we can rehabilitate plants. All we can do is to stimulate the normal processes within the organism itself. We seem to overlook the basic function of law and the significance of personal right and obligation in the creation of a society of secure and self-sufficient individuals.

We are criticized for stimulating the sense of dependency. Are we not properly criticized for so doing? There is only one proved method of avoiding the growth of the sense of dependency in company with any increased reliance upon proffered services. That method is to make him who is dependent the legal master of that on which he depends. The will retains its natural prerogatives when its needs are met through the exercise of a legal right. This is nature's method of avoiding the perversion of life's will in the face of its dependency. This is the legal method. It is the essential framework to which the administrative method should be subservient. To rely on the administrative technique without first creating a firm legal base of individual right and social obligation is like attempting to paint a picture without an underlying conception of it, a basic plan, or frame, to which the painting will give life and meaning. An administrative agency is an organism, having a coordinated mind and will. Like every other living organism it needs a basic framework of law against which to operate.

The majority of those engaged in the administration of social programs—indeed most of the representatives of these modern techniques, acting as they do under the impelling need for basic transformations in the social conditions under which people live—are liberal-minded individuals. From this standpoint, however, the law, while conservative in its approach to

3

change, seems to me in its basic philosophy quite as liberal, and, I am sure, even more sensitive to the need for preserving the freedom and independence of the individual, than any other social science. In fact, in a majority of respects, the application of legal doctrine to the very activities with which these professions are concerned, would seem to lead to far more liberal and objective points of view than these professions—and I refer especially to the profession of social work—have dared to adopt; for the members of this profession have been held back, not only by much popular (yet grossly false) creed and dogma, but by their own conception of the law as restrictive, as hamstringing, and essentially as upholding the arms of force and the police power. Many lack an understanding of the liberating force of the drive that lies back of our most freedom-seeking constitutional guarantees and principles.

At any rate, I must admit that my own thinking has led me to the espousal of a frankly liberal philosophy. I thus feel it necessary to stress the fact that these chapters represent the reactions of one who was thoroughly immersed in the conventional practice of law in New York City for about twenty years before becoming associated as counsel for Federal bureaus and commissions engaged in the administration of modern social legislation. Included in this later experience, however, are statutes in aid of education, child health and welfare generally, vocational rehabilitation, and social security. I was thus suddenly confronted in the very middle of my legal career with all these relatively new disciplines and techniques we call the social sciences, especially the applied social sciences.

These new disciplines spring from sources wholly foreign to the law. They represent an entirely separate tradition. They seem to have no important roots grounded in legal philosophy or principle. In fact, of all places, their representatives seem first to have met the minions of the law in the police court, and this without the advantages of any formal introduction. It

4

makes me think of the old legend in which a prince, who went hunting in peasant costume, met a princess also in peasant garb. Neither knew the true background of the other; yet in their blissful ignorance, so runs the legend, they at once fell in love. This happened in Nomansland, where the grim realism of our social problems was not a disturbing influence.

But the complete change of environment enjoyed by the author would be enough to prod the thinking of even the least imaginative mind. Two reactions soon towered above the rest. The first was a sense of dismay at the apparent lack of any draft upon legal texts, legal thinking, legal objectivity, legal science, in the actual training of professional personnel in social and welfare fields throughout the country. This seemed true even among those who acted under public auspices. There was a grievous absence of understanding of the law's objectives, some lack of respect for law that might in part be justified, a resulting failure to apply legal methods, and little awareness of the real contributions of legal philosophy to social objectives. There was, however, I must admit, a great longing for legal talent that could paint the law in less somber tones than they conceived.

I was impelled at once to pass in review what knowledge I possessed of law and legal science, to see how its most basic principles would affect the actual operation of social programs —of dealing with children, for example—their status, their treatment, their "commitment," and their placement. I reviewed the rules pertaining to professional relationships, the law's concern for objectivity of classification, the importance of what we think of as a legal personality, the importance of private guardianship, the tests of legal right and legal obligation. I came at last, somewhat dramatically, to conclude that if that most fundamental of our constitutional guarantees, that test of all justice, the equal protection of the laws, were ever actually applied to social programs, the whole field of public welfare would soon be revolutionized. The significance of the individual, idealized by social science, might then be on the road to realization.

My second reaction came later, at a more philosophical level, when I was forced to the conclusion that law, using the word in its most inclusive meaning, had but a minor influence at best upon the development of any one of the sciences relating to society, be it anthropology, biology, psychology, psychiatry, or some other sociological field. This discovery naturally led me to some fundamental research in what is known of man's pre-social history, of his primitive life, of the conditions under which he obtained his character and personality as a human being, of the relation between physical and human law, and of the conditions that made a society of human beings possible.

Through it all, I sought a way of defining law itself—law, as distinguished from government, from administration, from the police power, and from the exercise of authority—law in its most fundamental meaning where man's law and nature's meet—law as a science and as a philosophy. The whole field is virgin, for law, as an operating system in society, is so laggard that it seems to have permitted the very idea of a "social science" to be captured by disciplines quite alien to the law, until indeed a question arises whether law itself, as it is learnedly defined but not widely conceived in its social aspects, is itself a social science.

When you pass from the theoretical problem to actual operation in these public service fields, it seems to me that the legal profession rather than social scientists must assume the blame for the present failure to apply legal methods and legal principles. Lawyers, legislatures, and courts, rather than the social work profession, must assume responsibility for the failure to make these vital and extensive public welfare enterprises a part of our legally ruled and democratic way of life.

6

Legal Highways

Lawyers are at fault because they do not seem as yet to have caught the significance of what is taking place. Lawyers, it seems to me, must some day awaken to the fact that failure to invoke legal principles, failure to extend our legal system of rights and obligations into the field of public welfare, is causing a spreading sense of dependency and of social parasitism that has been the curse of many a political system before our own. Law should teach us that it is the fact of having a legal right to what we need, rather than the fact of having produced it or secured it by our own efforts, that furnishes the primary condition for preserving human dignity and independence. None of us in this day and age can satisfy our own needs; yet in a social environment, responsive by law to human life, we can still fulfill the Yankee's boast—"I ain't never had nothing that wasn't mine by rights."

Legislatures are at fault when, in order to meet some vital need of human beings, they see fit to appropriate a sum of money which has no relation whatsoever to the statutory objective or the cost of the service which the law purports to make available. They thus bring about a situation which is unresolvable by any legal principle, which gives no right or valid assurance to anyone, and the principal effect of which is but to extend the discretionary prerogatives of some administrative agency.

Courts are at fault because they have failed to apply the basic constitutional guarantees in the field of social welfare. Like a mirror they seem to reflect the popular conception of social programs as public charity—public charity, itself a conflict of terms and strictly speaking quite incapable of constitutional existence. Thus tradition carries on. Thus we continue to foster false notions that conceive our most significant efforts at social reform as a kind of charitable appendage to what we are accustomed to think of as our normal, legally ruled, and highly respectable economy.

7

The modern drive is of course for security as one of the greatest immediate needs of human beings. Only under law can both freedom and security be harmonized and equally promoted by the same rules.

Underlying it all is the grave possibility that human society, for whose creation the lawgivers of old will no doubt still be assigned a primary responsibility, is failing under existing conditions to constitute a wholesome environment for the formation and development of character and personality. Solutions are now being offered in rapid succession by the new disciplines. Yet one senses, perhaps, a clairvoyance in their diagnoses that unfortunately does not characterize their solutions. It is not hard under the circumstances to understand the failure to grasp the basic need of a legally ruled and legally responsive environment for the preservation of human character. It is merely to point out this primary need and the historical basis of it, as well as to advance a little the idea of extending our legal system of human rights and obligations so as to get law and applied social science more in step, that these few chapters have been written.

Chapter 2

FROM NATURE TO SOCIETY—THE SHIFT IN MAN'S SUPPORTING ENVIRONMENT

I LOVE TO WANDER around Mount Vernon, the home of General Washington. Jefferson's home, Monticello, is interesting, too, but Mount Vernon seems to me the very symbol of a free and independent life, a life that succeeded in maintaining a high degree of independence from the service of society. Mount Vernon was necessarily well staffed. Its looms and laundries, its stables and carriage-house, its gardens and food-processing implements and kitchens, its preserves of wood, its hunting equipment, its instruments of culture, even the broad river at its border—all were dedicated to the maintenance of life and to the satisfaction of life's needs. Shelter, food, fuel, clothes, transportation, recreation, cultural pursuits, every item of the social worker's budget, not forgetting the important "miscellaneous" item, could be checked off on the personal budgets of the inhabitants of Mount Vernon. Did it not represent the achievement of an objective in the way of independent living? Yet was it not an ideal to which the average family at the time might aspire, however short it might fall of the goal?

Now I have a little house in the semi-urban environment in which most people live today. The other night, as a cold wave was descending upon us, our automatic oil furnace failed to "come on" when the thermostat called for its response. Fortunately the telephone worked. The operator responded and I called the oil supplier, who in turn contacted an engineer on his staff. Four hours later, in the order of his calls, this expert arrived and gave us his diagnosis. The "atomizer" was clogged. We drew heavily upon this expert's ingenuity, for an oil-burner is complicated and delicate. It ages rapidly and needs much servicing. In the meantime, however, our attempts to substitute an electric heater had put all the lights out. A few hours earlier, the automatic gearshift in our automobile had failed, and this, I am told, was due to the breakdown of a solenoid switch. I would not know. I need an engineer—one versed in electronics.

Nor can I predict the ills of tomorrow from those of today. A filling gives way on a tooth. I catch a new type of influenza. A zipper refuses to lock. The milk sours on my door-step. A power breakdown throws the whole community into darkness and cold. A broken pipe floods the bathroom and the basement. I suffer from perennial shortages of needed gadgets. From such as this there is no refuge save in the resources of my fellow man. There is no retreat from society. There is no "simpler" life available. For most of us horses are out; wood is out; gardens are out; game is out; the west is out. The technics of civilization grow ever more technical. There is no salvation for us save in the responses of our fellow man. The "order of our calls" upon him becomes the inexorable condition of our daily living.

All life is dependent for its sustenance upon its ability to feed upon the medium in which it is conceived. It requires the support of its environment. It is neither self-supporting nor self-reliant. Basically the supporting environment of life is the physical world. But during the last one hundred and fifty years a profound change has been taking place in the nature of man's dependency. As individuals we no longer draw our support from nature. Human society, with all its complexities of social and economic organization, has intervened. We depend on our fellow men for what we need. What we used to draw from the ground we now buy from the grocer or from some other agency of our society. Review your own life from morning until night. See how few, if any, of your needs you can satisfy without the aid of other people.

Contrast the life of an adult with the life of a baby drawing his sustenance from his mother's breast. You will find there some analogy to the contrast between the present-day life of the average individual and his living conditions one hundred and fifty years ago. Then there were about one-third as many people on earth as at present. Over three-fourths of that population secured their primary wants directly from nature. For this purpose they learned to adjust themselves to its laws.

The population of the world is now increasing at the rate of about one per cent a year. To derive the significance of this quantitative increase one must multiply it by the mobility of the population just as the value of money is determined by multiplying the quantity by the speed of its circulation. Mankind has been tooled and implemented to increase greatly its capacity for the exploitation of nature; and in the use of their tools men have learned the technics of organization. The composite whole is a society of enormously augmented strength, and the result is that organized society—not government but the whole pattern of society and social organization—has actually interjected itself between the individual and his physical world and has become the environment of the individual from which and through which individual needs are met. Short, perhaps, of the breath one draws, there is scarcely any article of food, clothing, or shelter, or any service, or any of the manifold gadgets with which present-day society is implemented, that is not provided by one's fellow man and for the service of which one does not look to some organization of human beings.

To cap the climax you as an average individual have no power even to participate in this service or to support yourself, as the saying goes, except by establishing satisfactory relations with other human beings and cooperating with them. If you happen to be one of the sixty-odd million individuals who are normally in the labor market, you have at least a reasonable opportunity to do this. To be sure, earning capacity has not been actually assured of a steady flow of compensatory payments, but considerable progress by labor organizations, by unemployment compensation programs, and, on occasion, by public-work programs, has been made to this end. But if, on the other hand, you are one of the ninety million other Americans who are not in the labor market under the present economic system, and if you are not one of the relatively few capitalists, you are, in the main, thrown back for your support upon such relationships as you may have to a member of the labor group. You are thus reminded that you still depend upon a distributive system which, though it may have been reasonably adequate in times past, under present conditions fails to insure the meeting of the individual's needs.

The most fundamental of all rights is the right to life. To Jefferson, and to the framers of the Constitution under which we live, the right to life meant the right not to be deprived of life. The right to life was to them in very truth a "natural" right. For it was a life that God gave and nature supported. They thus built upon the premise that man's basic refuge was and would continue to be the physical world. Is not the earth the mother of all life? they argued. Nature has indeed met the needs of a living organism from the time when its capacity for "producing" what it needs is nonexistent, and when even its ability to draw upon its environment is as yet not fully achieved. The needs of life have been met from the very inception of life. Nature is irrevocably committed to the support of life, and this by the very terms of the laws that govern it.

But society is not so committed by law to the support of life. One of the first questions asked by the Social Security Board in Washington was whether an individual who might otherwise starve had under the common law any legal claim upon his community for bare sustenance. Blackstone pointed out that no such right had been conceived and "no compulsory method chalked out for this purpose." [1] The Social Security Act was an unprecedented initial step. It carved out certain specific categories of individuals, such as the aged and blind and some children, for the purpose of providing them with a basic cash income. The Act, however, contained no general acknowledgment of social responsibility. The individual holds as yet no general right even to his bare economic existence in our society. In the twentieth century the situation in this respect became anomalous. For while organized society was never so powerful, the satisfaction of the needs of its individual members was never more precarious.

What concerns me as a lawyer, however, are the deeper implications of this generally unimplemented human interdependency, this shift in man's environment from a world committed to him by irrevocable law to one in which he becomes subject to wills he does not control and which may be actually uncontrollable. What, for example, does this shift mean in terms of human character and personality development? For it appears to me that most of man's vaunted independence and boasted self-reliance emanates from his justified confidence in the laws of nature. In this context it is easy to understand why the withdrawal of the individual from direct and immediate recourse to nature's laws has left him profoundly shaken in his basic faith and in his morale.

1. William Blackstone, *Commentaries on the Laws of England*, Vol. I, Bk. I, *359.

The Right to Life

In the 12th Chapter of St. Luke you will find these verses: "And He said unto his disciples, Therefore I say unto you, take no thought for your life, what ye shall eat: neither for the body, what ye shall put on. . . . Consider the lilies how they grow: they toil not, they spin not; and yet I say unto you, that Solomon in all his glory was not arrayed like one of these. If then God so clothe the grass, which is to day in the field, and to morrow is cast into the oven: how much more *will He clothe* you, O ye of little faith? And seek not ye what ye shall eat, or what ye shall drink, neither be ye of doubtful mind. For all these things do the nations of the world seek after: and your Father knoweth that ye have need of these things. But rather seek ye the kingdom of God; and all these things shall be added unto you."

What did Christ mean? With our fondness for applying the rule of reason to biblical admonitions of this kind, we have sometimes satisfied ourselves that what Christ had in mind was merely to caution against an excess of emphasis upon the material aspects of life, or an almost complete preoccupation with physical needs. The quotation, however, is one of the most striking commands in the gospel. We must not mistake its meaning. I think Christ said that human beings could not afford to be anxious over their means of existence. They need to rest in childlike faith that the environment on which they depend is committed to their sustenance by the very laws that rule the universe and that it is utterly futile to be concerned about their effects. To live at all one must do three things—eat, drink, and protect oneself against exposure. Yet Christ said: "Take no heed what ye shall eat, or what ye shall drink or wherewithal ye shall be clothed." Then he took us back to nature. He reminded us of nature's commitment to life and of the glorious way in which it was fulfilled. It was nature's pleasure, its function, to conceive and maintain life.

Whenever I point out nature's basic commitment, its under-

14

lying guarantee of life, however, I am cautioned not to build too heavily upon it. This warning stems from an overemphasis upon the physical hazards of life. I am told society is concerned with the individual in a sense not manifest in nature. There is a feeling that nature gave life a run for its money, that it sacrificed individuals and was concerned only with the preservation of species, and that social science is mainly concerned with the relief of nature's inhumanity. Even the fact that nature is utterly incapable of hostile feeling, ill-will, or purposeful injury is discounted in our thinking, or is reckoned as naught against the magnitude of the challenge it offers to life's more extensive mastery.

But nature conceived and fostered life. To foster life means to foster individual life, for there is no life that is not individual life. Life manifests itself in its individual forms. Could I exist if I could not trace the life that is in me back, back, in an unbroken chain, to the primordial slime? Nature underwrote my life, undertook a basic commitment, and that commitment ran to me. To be sure, the advent of will, of conscious purpose and creative power in human beings has in its moral implications continuously revised our sense of values. The preservation of the individual has an increasing, an overriding importance in these terms. That which has now been produced is too precious, too potentially great, we feel, to be sacrificed otherwise than in support of a moral principle which stands sponsor for its immortality. But there is nothing in this effort to seek out, further, and exalt individual life that is not foreshadowed in nature's evolutionary designs, and while we may need to provide greater security to individuals, we cannot afford to do less. We cannot fail to find an adequate substitute for nature's firm commitment.

The hazards of life have played their part in its instruction; but they have not hindered the development of a healthy mind. Why? Because underlying the whole scheme of things, back of the universe itself, is nature's commitment to life. The simple fact is that the race has endured the hazards of nature with equanimity, and with a very wholesome mind, for life has always had a deep and abiding faith in its ability to command food, drink, and shelter. The native Siberian tribes, says George Kennan, lived mainly off the salmon that came up from the sea. Every so often there was a break in this cycle and famine followed. "No experience however severe—no suffering, however great, ever teaches them prudence." [2] What the author describes is not an inability to find methods of food conservation—a relatively simple matter—but an attitude of utter nonchalance. They refused to be concerned, and maintained perfectly sound mental health despite the physical hardships they endured.

We are wont to think of nature as hard and inhuman. Of course nature is hard and inhuman, for nature is law, not will, and lacks the power of wilful choice and discretion. But it is just that quality in nature, that hard and fast adherence to law, that has given rise not alone to man's existence, but to man's most significant qualities—his basic, underlying faith in himself, in the security of his existence, in his potentialities, and in his increasing independence and freedom.

My belief is that the key to some weakening of the sinews of individual life and character, some loss of poise and stability, indeed some loosening of our mental fiber, must be ascribed to the shift in the dependency of the individual from a world ruled by universal law to a world that is not thus automatically responsive. Life's dependency on its environment requires not only that its environment be responsive to the demands that life must make upon it, but requires also that its environment shall have no discretion under the rules that govern its behavior to do aught but respond to the demands of life upon it. It

2. George Kennan, *Tent Life in Siberia* (New York, G. B. Putnam & Son, 1870), p. 396.

must be automatically responsive to human needs because the laws of its existence make it responsive to organic exploitation.

Age-long existence in dependence upon such a law-constrained environment has bred into us humans a sturdy sense of independence, and of worth and prerogative, which dependency upon other human beings, unsupported by legal right and prerogative, has deeply wounded. God subjected nature to a rule of law that denied it any power whatsoever to oppose at will the demands of life upon its resources. Life could never have achieved its sense of mastery if its natural environment had possessed the power to resist the encroachments of life. The growth and development of human life is unalterably conditioned upon nature's inflexible subservience to law; for nature's subservience to law leaves it prostrate before the devices of the human will.

More than this, the Creator saw to it that this encounter between man and nature endowed man with a growing sense of independence in the face of his actual dependency. Independence results from the fact that the person or thing upon which we depend can do nought but serve our need. It is the function of law to convert dependency into independence. The Creator made human beings independent by yielding them the kind of prerogatives which rights under law alone yield. He used nature's unwavering obedience to law as a means of evoking the sense of dominance and freedom in the human will. The powers and prerogatives of life over nature became the basis of that sense of self-reliance and awareness of self which cries, "I got my rights" and "I ain't never had nothing that wasn't mine by rights."

One may inquire at length, though uselessly, into the quirks of thought which are loath to protect legally the dependence of man upon society at large while providing legal sanctions to fortify his dependence upon some other individual or discrete group having some particularized relation to the individual. The latter dependency is considered compatible with a prestige arbitrarily assigned to an attitude called self-reliance, while the other is deemed quite arbitrarily to be abhorrent to, or at least wholly inconsistent with, normal self-sufficiency. It is all very well, too, to say that we must habituate ourselves to this social interdependency and to the fact that our needs can be adequately met only through some degree of socialization of our resources; but that is not the ultimate answer to the basic problem of human society. It is the mind of man that you must secure, not his body, and the answer must be found in the fact that mental security has throughout the age-long existence of human life been associated with dependency upon an environment responsive to it by law.

The significance of this transformation will not, therefore, be found in its material aspects. The deeper significance of what has happened must be understood in the light of the teachings of eighteenth-century thinking regarding the repressive effects of social institutions on individuality. That society is doomed which does not enable human beings to express their normal and natural sense of mastery and dominance over their environment, to assert as a basic prerogative of life the right to command what it needs, and to enjoy at one and the same time both security of mind and freedom of will. Human beings must be enabled by law to make the same kind of happy, care-free adjustment and find the same kind of satisfaction in their life in society as they exhibit in "getting back to nature" or "down on the farm."

More is at stake than merely our physical and mental security. The moral principle itself is involved. For life subjects itself to no compromising pledges when it exploits its natural environment. Neither does it exhaust itself in so doing. It satisfies its needs but it is able to do so on terms that leave it free, at least morally free, to dispose of its fruits and to dedicate its capacities. For life has its two phases. Life has its needs and life has its capacities. As to the former, life demands security. As to the latter, life demands freedom. In the satisfaction of its needs life requires the security of an environment that has no power to do anything but follow beaten paths and predictable procedures. In the dedication of its capacities, life demands a freedom from compromising conditions. It must assure itself that it does what it does in the fulfillment of the moral principle. This sense of moral obligation is the healthy response of life to its prerogatives. The moral sense cannot possibly arise in response to any external compulsion upon it. It would not be a moral sense or a moral reaction if it did. The moral choice is the free choice. It is the normal reaction of life. The mind of man must be secure; but the will of man must be free.

It is not a mere question, therefore, of meeting the fundamental needs of life. The terms and conditions under which such needs are met will determine whether we are to promote the development of a healthy and dominant personality in our society or continue to undermine and destroy self-esteem and degrade human character.

This, therefore, is the first and greatest teaching of nature. This is the point of outstanding significance to us in the fact that nature is a wholly and completely law-governed system, whose processes are automatic, like the traffic light that replaces the policeman at your corner, or the "automat" from whose recesses you draw your food. For this characteristic of mechanized, autonomous, and self-regulating action is, you will agree, of particular importance in any system upon which you depend for your food, shelter, and other equally fundamental requirements of life. Should you come to depend for your very life on a system of conveyors, bringing food and clothes and drink within your reach, you would want that system to operate under as strict a routine as possible—free, so far as possible, both from the need for, and the likelihood of, any capricious, wilful, or whimsical interference. You would want it as firmly committed to its acclaimed schedule as is your own heart or God's sun. Least of all would you want it to require anything in the way of appeasement or propitiation as a condition to the continuance of its vital processes. If it did this, you would soon find yourself groveling in the earth, having pledged the last ounce of your pride and self-assurance and having perhaps sacrificed upon its altars even your very faith in the permanence of life.

The materialistic viewpoint, at any rate the belief that the necessities of existence are the underlying condition to the application of life's energies and productivity, rests on the notion that life was endowed with its capacities for the primary purpose of enabling it to meet its needs. Even plant life refutes this supposition. It draws what it needs but it produces what it does not need. It is made in the main to serve a life not its own. The apples that grow upon the tree are its free gift to life. But when you approach the order of human life, you are at once confronted with the fact that life is the embodiment of will. Its first requirement is a release from the sense of compulsion that is imposed upon the will when its own needs and its own survival are made its chief concern and the test of its sense of responsibility. For you cannot put a will under continued compulsion and still have a will. Voluntary action means literally willed action. Willed action is not compelled action. Life is not driven by its necessities. It is lured by its hopes. You could not satisfy or inspire the moral uplift and spiritual aims of life by directing it toward the objective of a more adequate meeting of its own needs. It demands what it needs on terms that, hopefully, leave it utterly free and entirely unprejudiced in the dedication of itself and its capacities.

I realize that I am skirting the basic point of cleavage between the so-called realist and the idealist. Some alleged realists say that if individuals had the assurance of what they need to keep them going, they, the majority of them, at least, would lie down and do little or nothing. Another group says that, by and large, they would build on that base—they would use their released capacities for constructive purposes, either to make higher economic ground or to achieve higher and more permanent values from their productive capacities. Others, and they may be in the majority, say no generalization is possible. It depends on the individual and no doubt on environment.

I wish to suggest a series of propositions. In the first place, life typically (and this means individuals typically) have steadily sought higher levels of living. This has not resulted from compulsion but from aspiration—not from what lies behind but from what lies ahead. Even those who work with animals may agree on this point. Education which provides a greater knowledge or basis of predicting what lies ahead will of course greatly accentuate this influence. If the necessity of existence was life's primary motif, life would not rise to higher levels. It often has a better satisfaction of its more limited needs at lower than at higher levels. It is characteristic of life that in satisfying its needs it creates more and greater needs. In the second place, the conditions under which life carries on rapidly lose their initial significance either as urges or as enervating influences. Life continually adjusts to its environment and goes on about its own business in calm acceptance of environmental conditions which, when they are first encountered, may greatly stimulate or depress it.

Then, too, let us remember we are speaking *of life and not of the absence of life.* We gain life and we lose life. Some have more and some have less; but we are justified in dealing with life as a fact in and of itself. Let us give more study to individuals who have life and who have it more abundantly. I think we will do well to deal with life from the positive standpoint, to study its ways and at any rate to be careful not to define it in terms of abnormalities and distortions. My further point is that in seeking better economic conditions, individuals seek at the same time the higher values that come with these conditions or that lie beyond them. There is no reason to stop at economic or materialistic incentives, for the purposeful human being is capable ultimately of conscious sacrifices of material for spiritual values, but only, of course, as he becomes aware of those higher ends and believes in them.

For all these reasons, and others like them, I conceive in the first place that a sense of security, a calm, undisturbed faith in the sustaining responsiveness of life's environment, fortified or justified by the knowledge of life's right to assert a claim to what it needs, is a basic condition to its progress. I would do what I could to remove from individuals all sense of being driven or compelled and endow them with the means of a richer environment, a greater knowledge of its potentialities, and, of course, insofar as possible, an environment governed throughout by highly ethical rules.

I am not impressed, therefore, with the conception of applied social science and the security drive which regards it as founded primarily on a growing humanism, a mere charitable consideration for human beings, or a developing social conscience. It is not that society is becoming tenderhearted. The motivation is far more profound. It rests ultimately on the gradual assumption by human society of functions formerly performed by nature. As the basic reliance of the individual shifts from mother earth to the organized productive capacity and distributive processes of the social-economic order, the individual needs a commitment by the laws of society that will provide the basis of as firm a faith in his existence as he had or believed that he had in the physical order—and upon the same terms.

Chapter 3

Man's Independence as Developed Under the Order of Nature

Recent studies of human history have been reminding us that many attempts to establish an enduring human society on earth have already been made and failed. One by one they have reached a certain stage of development and then have disintegrated and perished. True they have succeeded in leaving us with the vision of a far more effective social order freed from internal strife and capable of the kind of goals that can be reached only by a united and cooperative world. But at the same time their failure has served to remind us that we, too, even now, may fail. And this reminder comes at a crucial moment in our history.

The pattern thus revealed is coming to be fairly familiar. It would seem that as every great culture or society attains maturity the majority of its members find themselves more and more dependent upon its economic as well as its cultural organizations. The individual thus gradually loses the means of supplying his own needs in kind. He loses contact with his more primitive environment. The very form and nature of what he needs undergo fundamental change. Economic factors intervene. These economic factors are supported by a host of conventions to which the individual is required to conform his life. He thus gradually loses the sense of prerogative as well as the resiliency and *élan* that preoccupation with nature and nature's law has stimulated.

While this human interdependency has been dramatized in the present twentieth century, following the invention of steam engines and the resulting urbanization of our society, it is true to a lesser extent in other societies than our own. Neither in our own society, as we have seen, nor in any society to which we seem to be directly related, has this increased dependence of the individual upon his social environment been implemented through the creation of a corresponding system of legal rights of the individual covering the basic needs of life. The independence of the individual in society has not been guaranteed. Rome, with its high regard for law and legal forms, is a conspicuous example of the failure to protect the independence of individuals. The cry of her helpless citizenry for *panem et circenses* will be recognized as the symptom of Roman social disintegration.

Society has always been loath to obligate itself. On the contrary, the power motif in human society continually encourages the subservience of its members to the primary social organizations and to government. By requiring them to seek satisfaction of their requirements as a matter of grace rather than of right, they are made amenable to the demands of the state and to the ruling elements of their society. Human experience furnishes no basis on which to take issue with the conviction that mass dependency spells the end of a democratic political order.

At the same time the failure of society to underwrite the individual's basic needs is masked in society's reproach of the individual for his loss of self-reliance and economic fortitude. Thus, as so often happens in our thinking, we get the cart before the horse. We tend to ignore the rather obvious fact that the individual gained this same sense of self-reliance and independence during the uncounted centuries throughout which he lived in an environment that he himself could, with the aid of its laws, dominate.

Actually an individual who lacks an unconditional assurance of life is like an electric wire carrying a high voltage current without proper insulation. As the electric carrier lacking insulation yields its strength to the atmosphere, so human beings dissipate their energies in an environment which keeps them in subjection.. The primary difficulty is that society tends to engulf the individual. When individuals weaken, society disintegrates. The pattern of legal right and obligation which is intended to bind society together thus proves its inadequacy. The death of cultures is, therefore, due in my opinion to the failure of society to see that individuals are provided with the means of retaining their independence despite their constantly increasing dependency upon their fellow men. We need, I think, to retain this point of view when we examine our social and economic pattern. It should be our guide in all proposals to make that pattern more fertile and productive in terms of human character and personality.

Let us, then, do two things. Let us first see if we cannot identify some of those factors in the relation between man and his natural environment that have stimulated his urge to become a responsible human being; and then let us seek to review in some greater detail the relations between this same individual and his social environment.

I see before me a primitive man—but though primitive, still a man. This man knows of himself that he is a person, a being separate and distinct from all else. Aware of himself, he is also aware of what lies around him. He has learned to control and use some of these things. He makes them serve his purpose. He is able to bring about by his own acts certain conditions more favorable to his existence and comfort. He is therefore beginning to develop some sense of responsibility for those conditions.

But this primitive being is a member of no society larger than his own family. None such exists on earth. The human beings near him are blood of his blood and body of his body. They are as natural to him as the rocks and trees and bushes that lie around him.

What surrounds him is his own domain. Here lie the resources that support his life. These he can command, seize, devour, yet cannot reproduce. Thus he lives upon the breast of his mother earth. He is therefore both dependent and independent, dependent because if earth fails him he will die; independent because he can take what he needs and there is none to say him nay. The fruit upon the tree yields itself to his grasp. He has the will to grasp. It has none to resist. In contrast to himself, nature is but an order of events, day upon day, season upon season, fruit upon fruit.

Now this primitive man is one of a series of generations that leads all the way back from himself to the primordial slime. If it were not so, he could not be. Indeed beings very like himself, and with scarcely less in the way of human endowment than he, had lived, according to the best guess we can make, for perhaps a hundred thousand years, perhaps more.[1] But how many hundreds of thousands of years before that had nature employed in the construction of such a character and personality remains a question. For you see, man is a product of the ages. In these time dimensions society is but a fleeting development contrived by a race whose appearance on earth is attested only for a period of say a paltry hundred of our centuries. In no fundamental respect is man the product of his society. His society is but the recent product of man. We do

---

1. The Mousterian culture, for example.

26

not yet know what effects for good or evil human society is likely to have upon human nature in the long-run.

What then made man? What developed, within this familiar frame, capacities of character and even of well-developed personality, before ever there was a society upon earth. Whence came, during these countless millennia, the moral sense on which society was ultimately founded? The answer, of course, must lie in some aspect of the relation between man and nature, for it was in and out of nature that man developed. Back of both stands the Creator God.

Now nature means the order of nature, for nature is steadily being reduced in our conception of it to a system of laws. Nature is not merely governed by law; nature is law—precise, inexorable, even ruthless, but in any event sublime in the perfection of its adjustments—and this perfection of adjustment is proof in itself that nature is law.

So there you have them, man and nature; from age to age preoccupied one with the other—the nature that is law and the will that is man. In this unending encounter between man and the order of nature is to be found, it seems to me, not only the source of man's training and discipline but also the foundations upon which he constructed an ethical system. We would do well to establish beyond cavil the reason why this is so.

We will concede, of course, that there must be a germ before there can be a growth. There must be a beginning before there can be a development. The origin of man we may not know. But this does not prevent us from inquiring into the factors that have favored and maintained, or, on the contrary, may have harmed and stultified the development of man —not alone, or even primarily, his bodily development, but his character and will.

The starting point, as the experience of the race testifies, is that succinctly stated in the Old Testament. You will find it in the first chapter of Genesis, in the words, "To have dominion over all the earth." "Thou madest him," echoes the Eighth Psalm, "to have dominion over all the earth; thou hast put all things under his feet." This destiny, man was directed in the very beginnings of human law not to pervert. "Thou shalt not make unto thyself any graven image.... Thou shalt not bow down to them nor worship them."

Is it not presumable that the very awareness of self, the rise of the human ego, itself, is the primary effect of this intended dominance of life? Obviously, to say that I am I, is not merely to differentiate me from someone else. The image of myself epitomizes the whole history of the struggle of everyone that preceded me to separate himself from that out of which he grew. Each stage of that endless struggle for separacy, for movement, and ultimately for dominion, is reflected in the final ego that I, the egotist, finally became. Each success held its promise for the next. Each successful strategy with all its history of failure and ultimate achievement taught my struggling embryo what it needed for the next step, so that it gradually acquired more and more of the means and methods of exploiting its environment.

The living thing is only half the picture. You will not discover the dynamics of this development in yourself alone nor in any of the ancestors of "me" and "you" that ever have been. In every dynamism there is an active and a passive principle. So it is with life and nature. Life is the active principle, but the consequences of life's activities have been determined by the "laws" of nature. The output of the dynamism must be looked for in the reaction of these effects upon the man who performed the act. Whether the man hit a cocoanut with a stick or suddenly found that he had started a fire, the stimulus he received from the effects of his activities was obviously great. The consequences of life's activities in the rigid context of nature's laws give life its zest.

The importance of the passive element in the dynamism,

however, is commonly overlooked. Whether the writer be a psychologist or a biologist or an anthropologist, or even a zoologist, one may look in vain for a recognition of what nature's law—what nature's dedication to law—has meant to the making of the human race. I do not mean to say that these scientists lose sight of environment as that upon which life depends for its sustenance. What they often lose sight of is the character-stimulating role and function of nature's preordained and predictable responses. Anthropologists mainly deal with environment in physical terms. They are apt to suppress, in their zealous study of life's development, the contributions of the static field of the dynamo in which the wheel of life is turning. This oversight or suppression is fatal to an understanding of how human beings have come to be human beings. Human society could never have been achieved except by beings accustomed to the inescapable effects of law. Human beings have learned to act in a legally controlled environment. Their wills were developed, not in an encounter with wills equal or superior to their own, but in an environment controlled not by will but by law.

I think it has become fashionable to lose sight of law. I think this trend may be a result of the emphasis upon action and energy in modern times. Yet this very ability to release energy was the product of the earlier tireless study of nature's law in the abstract. For it is the rules of the game in relation to which life acts that challenge life. Whether the setting be simple or complex, it is still true that life, in the effort to attain its ends, must conceive its action in the light of what it has discovered about the answers nature will make. Life can do this successfully because nature's answers are pre-ordained and consistent. Because life's natural environment is bound by the rules, or, should we say, really is rule, order, or law in the ultimate sense, its answers are ideally consistent. Life's ability to predict them is a function of its own mind. There is no limitation upon man's ability to predict what nature will do except the limitations of his own mind.

It is customary to say of whatever acts consistently, "You can depend on it." What you mean when you say, "You can depend on it," is that you can and do depend on it without sacrificing your own wilful aims. This fact enables you to forget how dependent you are since you fulfill your own chosen aims and purposes despite your dependency.

Now here I am approaching the very core and kernel of my philosophy; for, in view of nature's consistency, life's dependence on nature is no more restricting than dependence on a railroad train which has no option but to run upon the tracks that have been laid down for it to run upon. Since the train has no capacity for whim or caprice, you can be reasonably sure of the outcome when you choose to ride upon it. To be sure a train must start and stop, and this might have the effect of introducing elements of uncertainty, but we have overcome that possibility fairly well by devising a printed schedule we call a time-table, which reduces even the startings and stoppings to a uniform procedure, to which the train's crew is adamantly committed. We thus routinize the whole procedure or, what is the same thing, we reduce it to law and order, and in so doing make it an effective instrumentality of life. To put it in every-day words, the train cannot spoil your plans by being wilful and obstinate. Having no will of its own, it is subject to your will. It is bound to help you carry out your plans, so long as they were made in the light of what the train would do.

So you are thus at once both dependent and independent of the train; dependent on it because you may have no alternative but to use it, independent of it because all that it is capable of doing is at your command in the fulfillment of your own chosen aims. When you use it, you preserve an unimpaired personal responsibility for your direction and destination. Its commitment is the basis of your freedom, but of course only within the limits of its capacity. As long as the train does not inhibit your freedom you cannot blame it for other restraints on your freedom that may exist. The track may not have been laid all the way to your destination. The train may not go as fast as you would like; but in all that it does do, it imposes no restraint. Whatever it does, it does in such manner as to extend your freedom of action. The train cannot inhibit you because it is strictly committed to the schedule which carries out your decision—a decision made in reliance upon its commitment.

The law characteristic of nature is therefore fundamental. It gives to life its sense of independence since nature's resources are committed to the fulfillment of life's aims regardless of the use to which life puts them. It gives to life its challenge since the good and bad answers that nature returns are always determined by the choices life makes. Finally it promotes in life a sense of responsibility for the outcome since the varying consequences of the alternative methods chosen by life are inexorable. To change the result life must change its method, and since nature's answers are always consistent, life cannot escape responsibility for the outcome. The plea of ignorance does no good. It has never been any means of escape from the rule of law.

This is all disciplinary, but disciplined life is the building material of which alone society can be constructed. I have never read a more convincing commentary on this point than that made by Dr. Kroeber in his comprehensive work on anthropology. Dr. Kroeber points out that the stone hand-axes, so significant a part of prehistoric culture, were fashioned by chipping—mainly, I suppose, by striking one stone against another. He shows how difficult a technique this was, and how ineffective, if the results achieved had to meet the competition of a slow grinding process, such as an ordinary mortal in

31

modern times might use. Dr. Kroeber points out, however, that the choice of the difficult chipping method was dictated by primitive man's lack of capacity for any concentrated effort over a period of time such as would be necessary to get results by the grinding process. Primitive man was capable only of emotionally controlled acts whose effects were direct and immediate.[2]

Man's capacity for prolonged effort was one of the products of self-discipline that took centuries or rather thousands of years for nature to bring about. This long period was needed in which life might come to appreciate and achieve the satisfaction of accommodating its activities to nature's subtler laws, envisaging, as it might, in the course of time more and more distant objectives. We are wont, perhaps, to think of this process in terms of intelligence and reason, but mind and reason are themselves dependent, obviously, are they not, on life's ability to restrain its own activities. Nature's job was to aid living beings in developing a capacity for predetermined and deliberated action. The mind is not the initiating agency. It is an auxiliary agent.

Now the ultimate reason for providing human beings with an environment ruled irrevocably by its laws is to preserve the prerogatives of man's will. A human being never loses sight of his own will. He is supremely conscious of it, supremely sensitive to its prerogatives, supremely aware of its initiating power. He is extremely touchy on the subject. He is instinctively aware of any threat to its integrity. He will see a policeman a mile away. He was born to have dominion over all the earth.

I pause a moment here for definition. The word I prefer to use is "will." I seize upon the term "will" as a means of expressing the great dichotomy—not the old dichotomy of mind

2. Alfred Louis Kroeber, *Anthropology* (New York, Harcourt, Brace and Co., rev. ed., 1948).

and matter which seems to have lost its peculiar significance—but the dichotomy of will and law. You ask me to define the terms. You will become peremptory in this demand when you read later chapters unless I can in some degree orient you.

I define the will concept very broadly. I mean the power to initiate action and the capacity for transmitting the influences that give it a particular direction. Indeed it comes to mean the power of expression, significantly in terms of ego demands. As such, "will" is a life force individualized and having its highest exemplification in man.

Law, on the other hand, describes the arena in which action takes place, or in reference to which the will functions and so permits a prediction of the effects or consequences of a given act or action. This, at base, is the supreme characteristic of what we call the physical order. To this latter "order" or pattern some ascribe the term "values" or "system of values." This term "values" derives its most concrete meaning for me as a lawyer when I think of the values that may be assigned to the objects in any arena of action—for example, a baseball diamond or a highway. It is in these terms that law is phrased. Thus law applies at social levels to the ethical systems that describe and prescribe the consequences of any action in the social "order."

Man plays the game of life upon the arena which God has ordained. The game, as I visualize it, is basically an encounter between will and law, or an interplay of will and law. Thus, as physical scientists have tended to reduce our conception of the so-called material universe to a system of laws, so perhaps I may be accused of attempting to "reduce" a very complex organic mechanism to some simple conception called "will." I plead only that there are here two concepts, "will" and "law," against the background of which it seems to me possible to state some valid and significant ideas that are of major importance to the integration of modern social-science thinking

33

with the existing, but dynamic, structure of human society—man-made society. These ideas I offer, as orienting to a lawyer who contemplates the newer fields of social thought or to anyone who considers the significance of law to these modern social explorations.

Let us return for a moment to our primitive man. I see him standing before his cave or nest. Behind him are members of his immediate family, bound one to the other by ties that nature itself has constructed like the ties that bind one unit of matter to another. They are as a part of himself. Before him stretches his domain. It lies prostrate before him and his demands. Then suddenly there appears upon the horizon another man—a stranger. That which now confronts him is another will, a power like unto himself, a being uncontrolled and unpredictable, able to conceive and act, with aims and desires that match his own. At its approach he beats his breast in furious emotion, for this is living confirmation of his deepest fears. This is no longer law nor is it self. This is another will —a supreme threat to his security. This is, indeed, his fellow man.

Primitive men, they say, were bathed in fear. No doubt they were, but fear of what? For every force in nature, there was conceived at long length a god; for every event another will, and that will was somehow figured as a person. Primitive men feared not law in nature, but caprice, emotion, anger, jealousy. They feared nature clothed in human garb. Aeneas is a good example. He was driven by force of the gods above on account of the wrath of implacable Juno. Wills and purposes and "animus" were seen where only law existed. The fact that nature was firmly bound to the pattern of its laws had not been discovered; so the objects of fear took human form. The unifying theme in man's conception of Deity, the one true God, came only with his awareness of the order in nature.

It was, of course, just this fear of will, of animosity, of potentially purposeful and intentional hostility, that the wise priesthood so skilfully exploited. Discovering certain physical cause-and-effect relationships having significance to the lives of the tribe, they developed the tradition of their authority on the basis of their assumed alliance with alien wills and personalities of mythical power. Knowledge discovered law. It disclosed at the source a creative will that had dedicated itself unalterably to the reign of ethical law. This in turn disclosed the real nature of Divinity, and the supreme trust reposed in human beings through the gift of will, with its power of life and death, and dominion over all the earth.

Compare, then, this encounter between life and law with an encounter between two wills. The two wills are two forces. Let us assume that they are directed upon or against one another. The two forces, coming together, must somehow merge. If they meet head on, the stronger force will presumably entirely absorb the weaker. The weaker of two wills may lose its individuality. A will that is in all things ruled by another will ceases, by the very definition of the word, to be a will anymore. In this event, since all human action is initiated by the human will, you have obviously achieved a destructive rather than a constructive result. If, now, you complete this picture by supposing a single human being to be struggling endlessly in a self-seeking environment of many alien wills and purposes you have painted a very hopeless picture for the development of either the individual's sense of mastery or the complementary sense of responsibility.

To convince yourself of the significance of this principle, compare your own reaction to a misadventure that arises from circumstances for which no individual can be blamed, with your reaction to a fate that only the wilful decision of one of your fellow human beings imposes upon you. Let it be not some single event like a storm or a cancelled train reservation, but let it be a continuing imposition that affects the whole

35

course of your life. Human beings are utterly courageous in the face of circumstances, however adverse, for they know, from the experience of life throughout the ages, that life will in the last analysis prove victor over circumstances. But from the wilful caprices of their fellow men, there is no escape.[3] The human will shrinks or dissipates its energies, beats out its brains in angry frustration before the capricious domination of another human will. The struggle of man with nature is always filled with promise. The struggle of will against will is destructive. Then let it be remembered that an individual is just an individual, and that his environment is the whole world that lies outside himself. What hope has he save in the knowledge that the ways of his environment are ordered by laws that are regardful of his person and its interests.

I think, therefore, that nature wisely arranged for a human being to mature in an environment shielded from the impact of other wills except such as were committed to his conception and service. When, through very gradual processes of family expansion, men acquired the capacity for fashioning laws and rules of ethical behavior that substantially reduced areas of conflict and introduced a community of objective, the possibility of human society eventuated.

But we need, I think, to remember that human society is still a bewilderingly new development in the life of the race. The history of society stands to the history of the race as minutes to months. The history of society seems too short, relatively speaking, to determine what its effect has been on the development of human character and individual significance. I am confused and bewildered that I do not find in current psychology any real recognition of the vitally significant fact that our main environment throughout the ages

3. "Men accept with equanimity the wrath of nature but become enraged when their own kind is the cause of their calamity."—Christowe Stoyman, *My American Pilgrimage* (Boston, Little, Brown and Co., 1947), p. 226.

36

has been nature itself, a routinized and predictable manifestation of the law and order that characterizes all natural processes throughout the universe. The tendency of psychologists has been to think of human character and personality as developing in the milieu of other people, of other wills and personalities. But this was not true of its developmental stages. In this regard I wonder if the eighteenth-century philosophers were not nearer the truth than we find ourselves today. For they evoked the blessings of our more natural environment, and feared the effect of men on man.

I am convinced that this view of our problem of living and working together has a meaning and significance far beyond that recognized by any writing in the field of social science that I have read. The other day I noticed in the usual melee of daily headlines an estimate that thirty million of us Americans needed mental treatment. Such warnings as these, whatever their motivation, whether exaggerated or statistical, are born of something pretty fundamental, so fundamental that it can be dealt with only in terms of an analysis of our basic reaction as human beings to our environment—and obviously not to our physical environment or any of its manifestations. All these have undoubtedly been present in the ages that have gone before. Factors have entered into our common experience to which we are not adjusted, or, I should rather say, to which we have not found the answer.

I find a suggestion of the cause in the approach of each of us to our fellow man, in our inability to suppress the dread fear of emotionally motivated forces around us—actually unresponsive to law, hence unpredictable—in the realization that we are utterly dependent on what they decide to do—and in the obvious fact that we are confronted in the daily expression of our wishes and needs by the din and dun of the "I wills" and "I won'ts" that unfortunately decide our hourly fate. It is the law of our being that we shall go forth and conquer.

Yet we tremble greatly and are afraid. In a sense our primitive nightmares, peopling nature with hostile wills, have attained an actuality of existence, for most of us are at present in all things dependent on our human environment, and this environment has not been made legally responsive to our most elemental requirements.

The shift in man's environment from nature to people has made the favorable responses of his fellow men necessary to his existence. They relate to the satisfaction of the elemental needs of his life, as well as to the safety of his person, and they strike therefore with telling effect on the days of his economic incapacity, on the children, and, of course, on the weaker elements of our society. The cry for security is not therefore a cry for indulgence but for our right to demand and secure that indulgence as a matter of individual right and prerogative. It is a cry to be relieved from the right of our fellow man to withhold or to condition at will the satisfaction of life's demands. We suffer from a great defect in our present environment, a lack of that faith-inspiring quality which has given life its very hope of mastery and of self-determination. The human race has suffered a very profound shock. It is not in a condition of satisfactory health.

This, I think, is the kind of orientation we need in our approach to the social programming of the future.

Chapter 4

SOCIETY'S FAILURE TO ASSURE MAN'S INDEPENDENCE
BY LAW

LOOK AT THE whole process of economic distribution. I am thinking of the means by which goods and services are actually allotted and made available to individuals. The distributive process is, of course, the passing out of money. The money commands the goods. The goods and services follow the money.

But the need of an individual for goods and services is not historically and never has been a determinative factor in the economic process. Mere need for goods and services, apart from a social security system, has had no influence at all upon the distribution of purchasing power. We get what our contributed capacity commands or exacts, not what we need. The distribution itself is normally made in the form of wages; that is, payment for the services of the individual. Some distribution of purchasing power also takes place in return for the contributions of property, as, for example, rents and dividends, but this is practically an exchange of property for property and is even less responsive to individual need than wage payments. The right to goods and services in our economy is controlled by the contribution of goods and services.

This is all set down in legal terms. It's our human law or

39

part of it, but is it fundamentally ethical or at any rate moral? Or is it wholly consonant with the function of society as the medium of human life? The notion that goods and services should be distributed in proportion to capacity and contributed skill rather than in relation to need is so strongly espoused that people actually contrast lawful right with need—that is to say, they come to regard it as inconsistent to define a right in terms that parallel need. A claim cannot be a matter of right and law, they say, if it is limited to and conditioned upon the need of the individual. Right, they say, is one thing; need, another. Need may be a ground for appealing to charity but not for appealing to law. And this remains true psychologically no matter how rigidly you may succeed in expressing your benefit scheme in legal terms. Let a lawyer explain in the clearest terms that a legal right is a legal right, no matter how it arose or what was the condition of its origin—just as salt is salt, for example—and he will still find people trying to put legal rights in prestige categories. An "earned right" is what I mean, they will say, though they must be aware that historically a property right carried greater prestige than earning capacity does at present. Earning power has only recently acquired influence. The ultimate effect of this philosophy is to belittle a right that is apportioned to the need of the claimant. Such prestige classifications are neither law nor science.

However, this popular differentiation between having something as of legal right and getting something merely because one needs it, strikes me as a most revealing piece of social psychology. It expresses no lack of reverence for law and legal rights. It merely assumes that it would be inconsistent to found them on need. Now law is conditioned on nothing in the world but the ethic it expresses. You can convert an ethical principle into a law on almost any terms you please if you follow constitutional methods of law-making. And indeed you will find that the American Constitution facilitates the process of seeking to express or establish individual and human rights. And as for ethics, I can conceive of none superior to that which establishes the individual's legal right to whatever *he* needs in common with all *other* members of the human race. How can you escape the conclusion that if need is to be met at all efficiently, or in other words, if there is to be an efficient use of the products that we make, there must be some influential factor in the distributive process that assures that actual need will be met before we ape nature's prodigality with its surpluses!

THE GRATUITY CONCEPT

Let me quote at this point from one of our state constitutions: "The General Assembly shall not by vote, resolution or order grant any donation or gratuity in favor of any person, corporation or association." Which state constitution contains these words does not matter, for this same prohibition in one form or another will be found in the majority of our state constitutions.

Public relief, or general relief, as it is called, has traditionally been regarded by the man in the street as the payment of a gratuity. It has been distinguished in this respect from such things as service awards, or a bonus in token of meritorious service, or a system of pensions to veterans. This conception has been carried over from so-called general relief to the social security systems of public assistance. The reason is, presumably, that these systems are financed by a general tax. The responsibility is thus socially assumed. As a matter of fact, the categories of public assistance under the Social Security Act are, in most public debates and forums, referred to as though they were part and parcel of the traditional relief system.

I decided one day to confront a class of lawyers, to whom I was lecturing, with this anomaly. I asked them how public assistance could constitutionally operate in this country. The class was completely at a loss for an answer. They had floundered for years in the milieu of public misunderstanding. None had ever really asked himself how these "gratuities" were constitutionally validated.

Of course, in some instances they were not validated. The usual rationale by which general relief has been sustained legally will be found in a decision rendered in the New Hampshire court in 1931.[1] This decision is historically accurate in assigning the function of relief to the police power as a phase of the laws of society dealing with vagrancy, the system of commitment as a public charge, and the old settlement law. However, the statute with which the new Hampshire court was dealing was what was commonly known as an old-age assistance statute. Categorical public assistance laws of one type or another had been passed during a period of about twenty years prior to the New Hampshire statute. In common with its predecessors, this latter statute provided for the payment, from the general treasury of the state, of certain sums of money for the maintenance of persons over sixty-five years of age who were without other resources sufficient to maintain the standard of living which it was the objective of the statute to underwrite. The statute reflected simply the system of tax and benefit payment, although, as the court noted, the law was impressed with various "safeguards" including provisions for the "recovery" of the sums paid wherever possible.

But what, after all, determines the constitutionality or unconstitutionality of such laws? Legislatures have from time immemorial appropriated money for the benefit of individuals who thereafter have found themselves unable to enforce payment of the sum so appropriated for them because the award was gratuitous and hence unconstitutional. State legislatures

1. *In re* Opinion of Justices, 85 N.H. 562, 154 Atl. 217 (1931).

have, for example, sought unsuccessfully to authorize the state treasurer to refund to public contractors amounts paid by them as Federal income taxes upon the amount of the profit derived from their contract. Appropriations have been made, unavailingly, to indemnify individuals for injuries suffered on the highway, injuries caused, no doubt, by the condition of the road. The courts have refused to require the treasurer to honor the draft in either case. The whole question was reviewed in the Supreme Court of the United States in a famous case [2] which arose because an earthquake had caused great financial hardship to a public contractor. An appropriation having been made to indemnify the contractor, the question arose whether the architect was entitled to his percentage of this payment as he, of course, was or would be if the payment was properly a part of the builder's contract remuneration. As this case attests, the decision in all such cases turns upon whether or not the legislature, in making the appropriation, was fulfilling a moral obligation or, shall we say, an ethical duty which existed independently of its recognition by the legislature.[3]

The system of public assistance is valid or invalid depending upon whether a fundamental ethical duty is recognized as resting on society—a duty which the Social Security Act and state public assistance laws were seeking to fulfill. As a matter of law, then, the legal issue is not affected in any way by the size of the group upon whom or against whom the supporting tax is imposed. All social security laws rest on the tax power and depend for their validity on the fact that the tax power is being used for a constitutional purpose—old-age assistance,

2. *United States* v. *Cook*, 257 U.S. 523 (1922).

3. E.g., a state court said: "The aid provided for in the act before us is not a mere gift or bounty, but is a payment by the state in discharge of a duty to a recipient who is entitled to it as of right, having established his eligibility under the act."—*Bowman* v. *Frost*, 289 Ky. 826, 830 (1942).

43

public assistance, unemployment compensation, and all the rest.

These considerations demand a far deeper understanding of the problem both historically and currently than is reflected in any debate upon the subject that I have seen so far. Under more primitive conditions the family had been the economic unit in society, and family law reflected the long-standing economic interdependence of the family membership. The same nature that supported plant life supported human life and enabled the family to achieve a basis of maintenance at the hands of nature in which all its members cooperated as a unit. But as more broadly conceived economic organizations took over the exploitation of nature and enlisted the services of individuals on a basis wholly unrelated to the circumstances of their family life, the problem of meeting the needs of individuals during periods of their lives when they were not so enlisted and employed became more and more significant. Blackstone, like many another, is an excellent legal authority but in no sense a seer. His diatribe upon the subject of the monasteries,[4] which he charged with the encouragement of vagrancy and mendicancy, serves today only to direct one's attention to the fact that Henry VIII, in expropriating their property, destroyed a much needed distributive channel in the economy of Tudor England. Queen Elizabeth learned this to her great annoyance. The need to protect the system of personal property, and the economy of her time, from disruption at the hands of the hungry beggars of whatever age and condition, formerly aided by the monasteries, motivated the Elizabethan poor laws, just as, in the third decade of our century, the threat to the integrity of the economic, legal, and judicial systems occasioned by the flood of mortgage foreclosures and judicial enforcement of other obligations, pointed up the need

4. Blackstone, *Commentaries*, Vol. I, Bk. I, *359.

for bolstering our own distributional system. And while the Elizabethan poor laws have been heralded as an initial use of the tax power to insure the maintenance of the incapacitated groups in our society, they exhibit far more obviously the use of the police power for this purpose than they do the use of the tax power. For Parliament did not itself undertake the fiscal responsibility, but imposed it mandatorily upon localities and local instrumentalities. The Elizabethan laws also initiated the family or relatives' support system, which, contrary to popular understanding, was not recognized by the common law.[5] This police power tradition was then carried over into New England, where it resulted in a series of statutory obligations, developing what are now generally known as family support laws and the responsibilities of the selectmen in New England towns and communities. Out of this development sprang the various historic methods of child indenture, commitment as a public charge, and the accompanying settlement and vagrancy laws.[6]

At present we have full employment with only sixty-odd million employed individuals and ninety-odd million other individuals. These latter compose our incapacitated and unemployable groups. All of us are members of these incapacitated and unemployable groups for a large portion, and most of us

---

5. The original Elizabethan Statutes are 14 Eliz. c.5 (1572) and 39 Eliz. c.3 (1597) revised and rewritten in 43 Eliz. c.2 (1601). Paragraph VII of the latter statute reads in part as follows:

"And be it further enacted, That the father and grandfather, and the mother and grandmother, and the children of every poor, old, blind, lame and impotent person, or other poor person not able to work, being of a sufficient ability, shall, at their own charges, relieve and maintain every such poor person in that manner, and according to that rate, as by the justices of peace of that county where such sufficient persons dwell, or the greater number of them, at their general quarter-sessions be assessed; ..."

6. Cf. the summary history contained in S. A. Riesenfeld and R. C. Maxwell, *Modern Social Legislation* (Brooklyn, N.Y., Foundation Press, 1950), pp. 685 *et seq.*

for the major portion, of our lives—and only a small portion of us have personal individual wealth which we can give in exchange for the calls which we make upon our fellow men. We must, therefore, come to see the system of statutory support laws for what it is; namely, a statutorily created system of economic distribution used as one means of carrying out the duty which society itself owes the individual, and which it seeks in this way to satisfy.

THE SIGNIFICANCE OF THE RELATIVES' SUPPORT SYSTEM

The English common law, of course, recognized no obligation of relatives' support. Generally speaking, it enforced no rule of family support whatever except the obvious ethical duty to maintain one's baby during babyhood and the duty of a husband to support his wife, which was essential, of course, if she was to survive in a common law country, where her separate legal personality had not yet developed. A great deal of the prejudice and misunderstanding exhibited in relation to social legislation is founded in ignorance of this fact. Most people are astounded to learn how limited was any support obligation imposed on parents. The English law did no more than recognize an ethical duty to foster the being one has created or produced until he can go about in search of his own food. As soon almost as a child could navigate by himself, English law, pleading its fear of condoning idleness, withdrew from the picture.[7] In the common law view, there is no basic ethic or moral obligation of support running with the

7. "No person is bound to provide a maintenance for his issue, unless where the children are impotent and unable to work, either through infancy, disease, or accident, and then is only obliged to find them with necessaries, the penalty on refusal being no more than 20*s*. a month. For the policy of our laws, which are ever watchful to promote industry, did not mean to compel a father to maintain his idle and lazy children in ease and indolence."—Blackstone, *Commentaries*, Vol. I, Bk. I, *449.

blood. The duty of support runs with property, not with blood.

However, following initial recognition of the economic, distributive problem in Elizabeth's time, legislatures have gradually extended the relatives' support system so that it often embraces even collateral relatives. But as legislatures have continued from time to time their efforts to make these laws effective, the economic system itself has become more individualized and family members have become less economically interrelated and interdependent. Thus we have ended by utterly confusing the blood relationship, in terms of which these statutory obligations are customarily framed, with the former actual economic interdependence of the individuals involved. As the economic premise, then, on which these obligations rested, gradually lost currency, efforts were made to bolster up the family support system with more stringent legal provisions. The criminal process was invoked, and effort was made to have employable members of the family sent back like criminals to their parental domicile. This method of trying to provide for the support and maintenance, as well as for the education and medical care, of the larger portion of society, has ultimately proved wholly ineffective because of its incompatibility with the existing economic system and its resulting inadequacy.

There is an obvious sense of frustration among those who may at any time be asked to enforce such laws. As applied to the maintenance and care of the older generation, legislators overlooked the fact that the original ethical basis for the support obligation was fast disappearing. The younger generation in a primitive economic setting became the inheritors of an economically self-sufficient establishment. They received their inheritance subject to the performance of a trust for the care of those who established it. The ultimate purpose and effect of these relatives' support laws, however, was to impose an eco-

47

nomic obligation on one individual to support another with whom he had no economic relationship. Law expresses social norms and gives them added strength and durability, but it exhibits no power to change the course of society's growth and development. It cannot even hold society to a particular method or pattern for long. A sufficiently obdurate attempt to do so by administrative authority will cause revolution.

Nowadays blood and economics are not enlisted together in a single enterprise. There is an analogy here between blood and economics and blood and citizenship. Citizenship is no longer grounded primarily on blood relationship but on the individual's actually living under the jurisdiction of a particular government. His allegiance is his own individual affair. The family in one form or another goes on forever. Hence as social patterns change, the family is found cutting across citizenship lines just as it is now often found that economic relationships are independent of family relationships.

The whole pattern of wage-earners and their dependent relatives is quixotic. Some families are highly prolific; others are well-nigh sterile. One poor wage-earner may have a dozen "dependents," while another with a greater earning capacity has none but a wife who is herself able to support him. The use of blood relationship is not a competent method of meeting the needs of the larger half of our modern society.

Up to this point I have been thinking not so much of a man's wife and young children, as of his parents and collaterals. The ethical duty to support the life you produce, unless and until other means of support are provided, seems fundamental. I have always believed that at the very least this duty and the right to such support should have priority over other statutory support claims upon the individual. But the obligations of a husband and father do not excuse organized society from its independently founded responsibilities. The child's right to life is not limited to his parent's earning capacity, which may be highly inadequate. After all, there are momentarily over two million children in this country who do not derive their support from parents except in some instances to a very minor degree.

Capacity is a relative term. The relationship it expresses is that between the power to bear a load and the load that must be borne. The trouble is that we always talk of individual need and individual capacity, whereas need, and capacity to meet need, are scarcely ever in balance in the individual case. On whatever scale you classify individuals you will find that the measures of need and capacity are inversely related. The periods of life's greatest need are the periods of its least capacity. This is a truism. The fact is we are all integrated parts of a single society of human beings. Obviously the true balance between need and capacity is attained only when you take all social capacity and all need into account. Individual rights must be written in terms of social capacity, not in terms of individual capacity.

But the point of ultimate concern to one who reveres the rule of law in the world is the role that this attempt to use relationship as the primary means of economic distribution assigns to government (and I speak here of government, not society), for government is here again dressed in the garb of a policeman with the duty not merely of punishing law violation but of compelling the individual to engage in a specific economic undertaking. It is not what the individual does about his relatives but what he does not do that sets the policeman at his heels. Now if it were a single act that you wished the individual to perform you might put him in jail until he did it; but instead you want him to enter into an economic relationship entailing affirmative obligations of indefinite duration. To do this, it is necessary for you not merely to pressure him but literally to by-pass his will. This is the role of superior force. If you want to make people do things involuntarily, and over

49

a considerable period, you must rob them of their independent wills. You must substitute your own will for theirs. You may achieve this temporarily by putting them in an administrative organization like the army, or in a vessel at sea, and thus involve them in a situation where their security of existence is dependent on "cooperating," to use a much-abused term. Hobbes in his *Leviathan* conceived all society in these terms. In his thinking people and government constitute a single administrative organization. A social worker illustrates this by citing the case of a young man, nineteen, who was called upon to support his father. His income was adequate. But since his father had deserted his family when this boy was a young child and since there had been great suffering because of it, the young man was of course extremely bitter. He stated plainly that he would not support his father nor could he be compelled to do so. He stated that he would give up his work, and would go to prison before he assisted his father in any way.

Nowadays we often grant assistance to individuals and then seek to recover the expenditure from their relatives on the theory that the obligation was primarily theirs. Assume for a moment that society should seek to foot the whole support bill in this wise. The security process then becomes indistinguishable from the levy of a tax upon a discrete group who are likely to be the least able to pay the bill. The system of recovery becomes a tax system that operates in reverse of the ordinary principles of taxation, for taxes are appropriately assessed in proportion to capacity.

Now at this point, I may be understood to advocate more charitable provisions for the underprivileged as they are sometimes called. That is very nearly the opposite of the point I wish to make. In fact I agree with those who think charitable dispensations are quite capable of breeding human beggary and what many call social dependency in its worst sense. Perhaps Blackstone was right when he said that the monasteries, in dispensing what was given and taken as pure charity, did just this. But if you make need the occasion for the construction of a legal right, then you no longer have "charity," you have a legal right; and if you have a legal right you are, in the popular psychology, independent, and if you are independent, what excuse is there for calling you a social dependent or a beggar or a parasite? If a right by inheritance makes an individual "independent," how can it be said that the receipt of other funds to which one is given a legal right, with an even stronger ethical foundation to support the right, leaves one socially dependent? He may have been dependent originally, but how can you say he is still dependent after you have made him independent—by law? Are we not confused by our preconceptions? It seems as though we maintained the charitable tradition and insisted that social security is a gratuity, for the express purpose of verifying our preconceived ideas of human parasitism.

RECIPROCITY OF RIGHT AND OBLIGATION

There are those who seek to justify the failure of society to underwrite the needs of its members by the very fact that our individual needs are so largely dependent on the labor or skill of others. It might be easier to recognize our mutual dependency if we conceived our problem as a mere matter of sharing what God gave us. Perhaps it is the fact that we all live on what a distinct group of us are conceived as producing which has made us so fanatical in apportioning our rights to our individual contributions of wealth, labor, and skill. The answer to this is legal ethic pure and simple. We shall learn to live together successfully when we recognize that our particular needs and the right to their satisfaction are normally and naturally independent of our capacities and obligations.

The general statement that we have no ethical right to the satisfaction of our needs unless we in turn dedicate our capacities, even if it be true, has no significance, nor has it any conceivable application to the specific case. Here, again, we are facing a very common misunderstanding of ethical principles. I believe that the greater part of the prejudice against social legislation springs from the dire confusion on this score. It is true, of course, that whenever you seek to emphasize the rights of the individual, you are asked to talk about his obligations. Now as a lawyer I am a strong believer in the importance of the individual's obligations and his development of a sense of obligation. I believe in the ethical principle that the individual's obligations extend to the uttermost limits of his capacities. But there are one or more basic points we need to get straight. An individual's rights are not conditioned, legally or ethically, upon his assumption or performance of obligations. I am aware that this is the reverse of what is repeatedly urged, but it is true nevertheless. Otherwise, you would do violence to the principle of the individual's moral freedom in the dedication of his life. You may insist that, taken all together, an individual's rights and obligations are mutually dependent (though even on this point I can find no support in the Christian ethic), but individually they certainly are not. If you come to me as a lawyer to have me help you enforce some right that has in fact accrued to you, I am not in the least concerned from that point on about your obligations. I am concerned only with the other fellow's obligation on which your right is founded. You may have obligated yourself in acquiring the right; but it is quite as likely that you did not. Rights and obligations, you see, are not words of individual import. They are words of social import. The right is in one; the obligation on which it depends is in another. No one can have a right unless someone else has an obligation, and no one is obligated in the abstract. His obligation will be found in another's right. As applied to the individual himself, this means that the ethical basis for individual rights and the

52

ethical basis for individual obligations are distinct and not mutually dependent. The ultimate basis of the right to what life needs is life's dependency upon its environment. This requires that a right be created so as to effectuate life's prerogatives. Obligations, on the other hand, rest ultimately upon, and are measured by, capacity. Christianity teaches us that there is no limit, from the ethical standpoint, to the acquisition of rights or to the assumption of obligations. This seems to me to be implicit in the supreme sacrifices of life which the Christian ethic demands, whereas that same Christian ethic assures us that we are unconditionally worthy even of such a sacrifice as was ultimately exemplified in the death of Christ upon the Cross.

There is an obvious reason for the fact that the conception of society's obligation to the individual has yielded in our modern culture to an emphasis upon the individual's obligation to organized society or to his government. Personalized loyalty to the state was the essential means whereby the state at length triumphed over the more primitive but instinctively strong tribal bonds. Great state builders have uniformly promoted the cause of state allegiance, as, for example, through the identification of political and religious symbols. They have made capital out of the fact that family loyalties yield only to impulses and constraints that have a religious significance for the individual. By establishing the individual's primary allegiance directly to the state it became possible to regiment mankind and to construct the great power mechanisms of today. Individuals were organized in groups with uniform characteristics, especially by age and sex, to make them the implements of will and force.

We need more than anything else to reverse this whole trend. The family, of course, is an organization of individuals of varying age and opposite sex, firmly and instinctively bonded one to the other through the attraction of opposites, and providing therefore an individually secure and socially stable unit. The family is historically disdainful of citizenship lines, as indeed it is of many other differentiating characteristics. Since more effective agencies of social stabilization are the immediate need of modern society, the heightened prestige of the family is an important social objective of today, for we know as a matter of history that if our society does continue to yield its strength in a strife from which it cannot soon recover, the family may once more become the sole reliance for a new social reconstruction.

We seem, in fact, to be gaining an acute awareness of this need for the family in the crisis that confronts us. The rise of the security motif reflects the concern of organized society with the fulfilment of those basic obligations which until recently had been achieved through the united efforts of the family in the exploitation of natural resources. In a sense the earth did not support individual life directly but it did so through the medium of the family. This way of life is past and gone, but the yielding up of the economic functions of the family vis-à-vis its individual members demands in its turn the substitution of a basic responsibility for the economic welfare of the family membership on the part of organized society.

And from the standpoint of organized society itself, it is quite as important that society should be able to enlist the full capacities of its members, when in the individual case they attain high tide, as it is that an individual should be able to exercise his rights at a time when his capacities are virtually nonexistent. Just as an individual's call is upon all society, so the call of organized society is upon all its members. If society were forbidden to charge individuals with obligations that required them to exert themselves to the fullest extent of their individual capacities—if society could demand of an individual only such effort as he would have to put forth to

54

meet his own needs at a given moment—society would be unable to provide for the common weal.

Yet it is only gradually that the principle of taxation in proportion to ability to pay has been generally recognized and applied. It used to be the rule that a tax would be levied only upon those who benefited from the purpose for which the tax was imposed. The school tax is a good example. It was separately imposed on families having children of school age and was therefore related to the compulsory school attendance law. Nowadays the income tax process has familiarized us all with the principle of taxation in accordance with ability to pay. And the principle has gradually affected all tax measures and computations.

The apportionment of obligation on the basis of capacity imports as a true corollary the establishment of rights in relation to the needs of mankind. In fact, the one follows normally from the other. The need of society for an educated membership taught us this principle. When you reverse this sequence and insist that contributed capacity is the proper measure of an individual's right, then need becomes a measure of obligation. It does so in fact, for the feeling that need is the basis on which obligations are undertaken is the natural accompaniment of such a conviction. There is a widespread belief, too, that this harsh and unethical system is necessary to the discipline of mankind. Actually, however, we are disciplined only by having to live in an ethically ruled environment.

CRITIQUE OF EXISTING SOCIAL SECURITY CONCEPTS

These principles must lead one to consider briefly the logic of our Social Security system as it is currently envisaged. It may be clarifying to start with an individual actually in the labor market, ready, able, and willing to work. The compensatory return to the individual by reason of his abilities and contribution would seem to be the appropriate subject matter

55

of insurance in the true sense of that term. His current ability to work is a thing of value for insurance purposes, and if he finds himself for some reason out of work temporarily or is under some temporary disability or illness and is therefore not in receipt of wages for a period, the insurance underwriter may properly be called upon to make good all or a part of the loss arising from the individual's having suffered one or the other of these hazards. Thus, what we now call the unemployment compensation program would seem to be a strictly insurance program, call it social insurance or what you will.

But when you come to the living requirements of the old-age group, the child population as a whole, and the disabled, you have a very different situation. Regarding old age as itself a hazard to be insured against has always seemed to me a little like insuring the deacon's shay after its hundred years of service is over, or like insuring a house at the end of its economic life. The ultimate objective of a security system is to assure the meeting of the needs of what appears to be the major portion of our population. Recourse to the productive capacities of society as a whole seems logically requisite to do this at all satisfactorily. You may by deduction of a reasonable amount from the pay envelope of an individual provide for the individual himself in his old age. The justice of imposing this obligation upon the industry in which he is employed has constituted a powerful argument in support of the old-age and survivors insurance program. When you attempt, however, through this fund, to meet the needs of all those who are not for the time being economically productive, you are at once confronted by two major problems. One is to see that equitable provision is made for the dependent population individually, notwithstanding the quixotic elements that determine the extent of this derivative burden in the particular case. The other is that you are confronted with the fact that large groups of aged individuals, children, and disabled persons cannot, under the system of intrafamilial obligation, trace their dependency to anyone in the labor market. You meet the first of these problems, as far as the system permits, by spreading the burden throughout the contributing group. But spreading the burden is not limited, as a technique, to insurance. It may be conceived as an aspect of the much broader concept of what may be called socialization, or the mere pooling of resources as a means of cooperative financing. A draft on all productive capacity is needed to meet the second problem. The needs of those at the opposite end of the scale from the economically productive group are often greater because of their physical or mental condition. The best capacity is essential to meet the greatest need. Your draft must ultimately fall upon all society, that is to say, upon its utmost capacity.

In the attempt to meet these problems you are faced with the current political and economic philosophy which has resulted in the imposition of a tax only upon the first few thousand dollars of earnings. The constitutional basis upon which the contributions are assessed is, of course, the tax power, as the Supreme Court of the United States has held,[8] but the economic basis of the assessment closely resembles an annuity purchase. This conception of the pay-roll levy as an annuity premium is, of course, emphasized by those who think that individuals cannot or should not lose a stimulus derived from the belief that they are meeting their own needs rather than the needs of others. The resulting levy is not only regressive but insufficient in many instances to justify the conclusion that the individual has really earned the benefits that are payable by reason of his employment. In the case of the group with low earnings, the conclusion of self-help becomes progressively more fictitious. To satisfy the real objective of meeting need, the benefits have to be raised for the low-earning group by

8. *Helvering* v. *Davis*, 301 U.S. 619 (1937).

57

assigning wholly artificial values to their earnings,[9] whereas the benefits are cut off at a conservative upper level to protect the fund by restricting the draft upon it to the meeting of what in the normal case would prove to be actual, if not dire, need. Obviously, as you expand the coverage for the purpose of meeting the economic needs of more individuals, this characteristic must necessarily grow likewise. The system must increasingly tax capacity as it is extended to areas of greater need and incapacity.

The real objective and the necessary conditions to a meeting of that objective become clear only as the scope of the security undertaking is actually broadened. That is, what you are actually doing or seeking to do becomes apparent only as you extend or "blow up" the security system. As you gradually enlarge the program so as to approach universality of coverage, in the sense that all not currently benefiting become contributors and all become potential beneficiaries, it then becomes apparent that a tax is being imposed on productive capacity (which of course should be imposed in proportion to capacity, after the manner of a tax) to meet the needs of those not properly in the labor market. In other words, you will, by the slow process of enlarging the insured group, gradually reach the point at which all are taxed and the obligation is once more socially assumed as is the case with public assistance. And the achievement of universality and legal equality lies at the very heart of government function.

The resultant system is social security, whether it be de-

9. As the law presently stands, a total tax contribution on the part of the individual employee of $6 paid with respect to six quarters of minimum earnings can result in benefit payments aggregating $16,300, in which case the tax-benefit ratio is something less than 1/100 of 1 per cent. Moreover, a widow's benefit payable to her after she reaches the age of 65 years has a $30 minimum, and the family monthly benefit to a widow and children may not be less than $50. Thus, need is seen to be in actual fact a prime factor in benefit determination.

scribed as public assistance or social insurance. It would differ from existing public assistance only in its scope and in its provision of more objective formulae in the determination of the amount of the individual benefits. This last is a factor of prime significance in the creation of legal rights, cognizable by a court.

The contention that actual need has not thus been made a factor of control in the distributive process, however, is not valid, for the benefit formula must be such as to meet the needs of the least capacitated and of the lowest wage-earners. In fact, we all must live; and in order to maintain a satisfactory minimum standard, need must be a factor of control, for the system cannot sustain the burden of economic wastage or an unnecessary use of the tax power. There is, moreover, no reason to insure socially those who, in a capitalistic regime, have adequate recourse personally to capital. As for psychology, you would do better, it seems to me, to rely on the prestige that accompanies any well implemented legal right than to keep harping on the idea that earned rights are better than other rights. Society seems always to be the victim of the prestige values it assigns to economic capacity, whether it arises from royal grants, possession of property, or earning power. If we believe that individuals should be encouraged to face reality, why bid them cloak their needs in a fictitious garment attributed to the magical loom of insurance?

The current psychology is doing great mischief. For as you expand the social security system—I mean the so-called old-age and survivors insurance system as distinguished from public assistance—emphasizing with each expanded step that the individual is "earning" any benefits he receives, you are at the same time subjecting those without earning power to a more and more poignant self-condemnation as social parasites. The psychology thus induced will ultimately prove disastrous to

59

society's attempts to rehabilitate the individual and reconstruct interpersonal relationships.

A gratuity is a gratuity only because it is not a legal right, and charity is charity only because it is not law. But do not then argue that what has been a gratuity cannot be a right or what has been charity cannot be law, because in your very description of what has been, you have provided the legal draftsman with a sound ethic, and being thus provided with an ethic, he will thereupon incorporate it into a law. As soon as he has done so, it will be perceived at once that what you have received is not charity at all, but a highly respectable legal right. What you have received—call it public assistance—will now be found described by the courts in language of the following sort: "This is rightly considered, not as a benevolent gift but the fulfillment of a legal and moral obligation," [10] and "the aid provided for in the act before us is not a mere gift or bounty, but is a payment... in discharge of a duty to a recipient who is entitled to it as of right." [11] Thus spoke the courts concerning public assistance.

The New Testament is replete with evidence of the fact that the ethical compulsion of human need is greater than the ethical duty to fulfill contractual obligations. In Christ's parable of the prodigal son, the father said to the elder brother, "All that I have is thine, but... this thy brother"—and in another parable, to him who had labored in the vineyard all day long, the owner of the vineyard said, "Friend, I do thee no wrong; didst thou not agree with me for a penny?"—And he added that he was not thus to be deterred from making a similar payment to others although their earnings were far less.

The translation of an ethic of benevolence into a statutorily affirmed and constitutionally guaranteed legal right is of the

10. *Sacramento Orphange and Children's Home* v. *Chambers*, 144 Pac. 317, 25 Cal. A. 536 (1914).

11. *Bowman* v. *Frost*, 158 S.W. (2d) 945, 289 Ky. 826 (1942).

very essence of the security problem, as it applies to those whose sole reliance it becomes. It is not good either for the individual or for society that its members should obtain assistance by begging for it. It is of the very essence of democracy that the ethic on which we rely shall be embodied in our laws. Social security, to fortify the hearts and minds of men, must be established on a basis of legal and financial certainty, for merely seeing to it that human beings do not lack the requirements of decent living is by no means the end objective. In order to restore the basic confidence of the individual in modern society and give him the proper sense of his own security, the system must be conceived as a part of his normal legal environment and not as a smug social prescription wherein to drug the sense of human inadequacy and personal failure. We must regard the quality of legal rights quite as highly as the quantity of economic rights. Mental and emotional security can only be assured by the fact that we live in an environment responsive to us by the very laws that govern its behavior.

Chapter 5

Human Perversity—Society's Excuse

Community attitudes in relation to social measures are colored by a conception of the individual's relations with society and society's relations with the individual which is very bad psychology. We know a good deal more than we used to about people, but we sometimes get our plus and minus signs reversed—like the young astronomer who was assigned the problem of determining mathematically the position of a certain star. He performed the operation accurately save only that, by interchanging a plus and minus sign, he located the star at the precisely opposite side of the universe from where it is. Many fail to see that society is often kicked at by the individual, who acts like a frustrated child because he is being asked to supply what society itself has taken from him, and is withholding from him, and because its return to him is sought to be conditioned on his good behavior.

Individual behavior has literally no merit whatsoever as an excuse for society's failure to promote individual security; because human security rests on human rights. We do not give rights to the righteous and withhold them from sinners and parasites. If we did this, the rich would be gravely afflicted, and the idea of legal equality would be forever forsaken. The

62

fallacies on this subject, spread daily over the pages of our public reading matter, blind people to the truth. Like all exhibitions of prejudice, they rest on premises that could never stand or gain acceptance were they openly stated. Their validity is implied, however, and they are assumed to be the obvious conclusions of human experience.

I read recently an editorial in a leading newspaper that fairly gushed from start to finish with this kind of false psychology. A central theme was that public welfare departments should see that rent, and gas, and electric bills are dutifully paid by those whom the tax power is used to maintain. Admit whatever lies behind this statement, one would still ask why landlords and public utilities should not collect their own bills. They are much better qualified to do so than is any social agency. One would suppose from the editorial that the failure to pay such bills was costing the public money. If the recipient is merely given a legal right to a maintenance income on a periodic basis and at a fixed standard, it will not, of course, cost a penny to let him manage his own affairs. Regardless of what he does with his money, the amount he receives will be the same. True, we all find that our profligacy will hamstring us when the pinch or emergency develops a few days or weeks later on. We may find that our earlier decision carries with it a sacrifice we do not relish. But our lack of foresight does not necessarily consign us to perdition. The situation is not inflexible granted some reasonable regular income. When emergencies arise beyond the capacities of such an income as when it involves a major surgical operation or extended illness, our call is upon a service other than that which lies within the objectives of a normal security or assistance income.

In utter contempt this editorial went on to excoriate the social process because unworthy persons are on public relief—so-called. They probably are, as they are on many a pay-roll or list of stockholders. But what does the writer mean by "unworthy"? That the individual was employable? Then give him the command of a job and training to overcome his handicaps. Does he mean weak and irresponsible? Life's greatest stimulus springs from its prerogatives. You will not strengthen the human will by suppressing it. Does he mean that the individual is a law-breaker? Denial but adds to the attitude of social hostility.

I think here of the lady who wanted her pink satin quilt reserved for a "worthy" baby.

The truth, of course, still stands. The higher the ethical plane on which laws are written, and on which society acts, the greater the response of the individual. There is but one sound rule—to see that the legal base is ethical, stripped of all punitive motivation. Achievement is stimulating; failure and defeat are not. You cannot raise an aeroplane by weighting it down or by opposing it, for the strength of the engine measures the limit of the opposition it will overcome, and that opposition the engine itself is quite capable of producing by an unalterable law of physics. The more powerful the engine, the more opposition it will create for itself, but only such as it can overcome. Action and reaction are equal when law reigns. All you can do effectively is to build better engines and treat them well.

The human will, faced with law, is required to make choices, and he who makes a choice must abide by its consequences; and this is disciplinary. But the discipline that results within the mind is turned to poison the moment that wilful insistence is substituted for the circumstantial, or at least logical, consequences of one's own choices. The human mind is a perfect mine detector, a perfect radar detector in its ability to sense the presence of insistence. Necessities that appear to grow from circumstances we accept. Insistence we reject. The legal draught derives its poison from the cup of force with which it is served. We are all extremely sensitive to hostility.

No effect or consequence is disciplinary save to the extent that the laws that produce it are utterly devoid of all wilful demands and pressures.

When the will of one individual becomes wholly selfless and motivated only by its concern for another, it will say, "Not my will but thine be done." It will abdicate its own prerogatives and serve and work through the other will. This is indeed the professional and spiritual approach to human weakness and must be treated as a strength-yielding method. Obviously this method must proceed by establishing a harmony of wills, since every divergence of aim, every pulling one against the other, neutralizes and dissipates the energies that are needed to reinstate the individual's sense of mastery.

How interesting it would be if the Congress of the United States should establish, in the language of a recent high school debate, a comprehensive system of free medical care for all citizens of the United States, provided, however—and here's the rub—that none of the services or benefits so established shall be available to any individual who upon due investigation is found to have brought about his condition of illness, disease, or incapacity through his own carelessness, wilful misconduct, or any vicious habit whatsoever.

Obviously, we would be in for a more or less universal inquiry into all the manifestations of human weakness and depravity. But do not suppose for one moment that, apart from its broad scope, this provision would be without parallel or precedent. Quite the contrary is true. It would indeed be the logical culmination of statute after statute which has been passed for the declared purpose of promoting the welfare of society. The regulations governing pensions to veterans following the text of the Federal statute have provided that no pensions would be payable under Part 3 of the Regulations for any disability due to the claimant's own wilful misconduct or vicious habits. Section 710 of Title V of the United States

Code dealing with Executive Departments provides that retirement annuities by reason of disability shall be available only if the disability shall be found "not due to vicious habits, intemperance, or wilful misconduct on the part of the employee." Similar provisions will be found scattered through the laws of most states of the Union—but not necessarily in relation to health or disability laws. For the whole pattern is founded upon the existing and traditional provisions of relief, assistance, and security dating back through the years. You can easily find at least fifteen different behavior conditions in public assistance laws, extending all the way from a failure to pay legitimate obligations, an investment in or display of articles of luxury, idleness, drinking, or merely living in what has become a byword among social workers, "the unsuitable home." If the principle of this legislation is correct then nature itself is wrong in its attempts to establish the individual's sense of personal responsibility for his behavior; for the fruits of nature are not yielded on the condition of good behavior. Life can never survive the relinquishment of its prerogatives of self-determination.

What a curious misunderstanding of human beings, and of governmental function as well, is portrayed when public welfare administration is publicly condemned for continuing to provide assistance to individuals who indulge themselves in some one or more of the common vices of mankind! What this point of view seems to me to propose is to authorize a code of behavior—a code more exacting than our criminal codes have ever set themselves to enforce—to be drawn up, not by legislative process, but by a public administrator in his office. Upon drafting this code, the administrator is then expected personally to judge the behavior of the individual on these terms, and upon finding to his own satisfaction that some provision of this code has been infringed, to withhold from the alleged delinquent the commitments of society undertaken to sustain him or develop his potential capacities. If this procedure does not negative all that the Bill of Rights stands for, what does? Such a proposal rests on the firm premise that the individual has no right to command the support of his society, and cannot therefore obtain it except upon the condition that he yield prerogatives of freedom dearer to him than life itself. This theorem must fall before the facts at the foundations of all human life.

Law is not to be conceived as an agency of reformation. It has no purposeful goals of its own devising. We should somehow confront the individual with a framework of passive law that seeks no credit, no glory of its own, but merely provides for life its backgrounds and the means of its advancement. This is all that life has ever demanded. On this basis it has flourished.

The prostitution of human rights which occurs where their exercise is subjected to behavior conditions is tied, hand and glove, to authoritarianism. It simply attests the police power origins of social welfare legislation, because police power concerns itself with the individual's behavior, whereas the tax power touches only his property.

Prior to the enactment of the Social Security Act, the courts, seeking to classify "relief," and later the public assistance programs, as a governmental function, veered from the police power to the tax power. To some judges the issue posed by the attempt to have them declared unconstitutional, was merely whether the tax power was being used for a public purpose. Others who, like the New Hampshire court,[1] assumed the payments to be gratuities, found that they could be constitutionally validated only as an exercise of the police power. This is one of the most intriguing phases of the history of the judicial concern with public assistance.

---

1. Opinion of Justices, 85 N.H. 562, 154 Atl. 217 (1931).

The broad distinction between the police power and the tax power is clear and unmistakable. As defined by leading authorities[2] the police power is a means of promoting public welfare through restraint or regulation. The police power is not used merely to raise money. The police power reflects the exercise of authority. Its mandates usually impinge directly upon the will of individuals. Reliance upon police power concepts, however, in measures adopted to promote the public welfare dates back through the Elizabethan poor laws, to the earlier statutes to suppress vagrancy and quell social disorders and other unsocial behavior related to hunger and poverty. Later the power was similarly employed to enforce the settlement laws and, as we have seen, to procure the support of individuals by relatives and by local communities. This police power involvement reflects the motivation of public welfare measures to keep the peace and maintain order in the community rather than to benefit the group affected by the welfare law itself, as would ordinarily be the case with a social program which rests on the tax power.

When the Social Security Act was enacted, it was necessary for the court, in upholding the Federal social security system in relation to individuals over sixty-five years of age—so-called old-age insurance—to resolve this issue in favor of the tax power as the only available Federal constitutional power which could be invoked in support of it. In general, the Federal government can exercise police or regulatory powers only in the effectuation of one of its delegated powers. The Supreme Court decided that the Federal Social Security Act, in those respects wherein its constitutionality could be tested, invoked the tax power for a public purpose. The decisions thus rested social security squarely on the tax power. In so doing they also by implication repudiated police power conceptions of

2. Ernst Freund, *The Police Power, Public Policy and Constitutional Rights* (Chicago, Callaghan and Co., 1904), § 25.

public assistance. For, though no direct test of the constitutionality of the public assistance titles could be framed within the jurisdiction of the Federal courts, it remains, of course, true that they are supported at the Federal level by a general tax. The fact that the tax which supports public assistance is not levied merely upon individuals who may become eligible as beneficiaries under a concurrently enacted benefit program is, of course, an argument for, not against, its constitutionality. Obviously, this is a pure exercise of the tax power and, obviously, the power is being exerted for a public purpose. But the drafters of the Social Security Act felt it wise in the case of old age insurance, as also in the case of unemployment compensation, to separate the tax titles (old Titles VIII and IX) from the benefit provisions in order to make it appear that the tax power and the benefit or welfare power were being employed independently of one another, and to prove in this way that the drafters were not putting the Federal Government into the business of regulating or policing employment. The latter objective would, of course, render the statute unconstitutional. Obviously, however, the more general the tax and the more closely it is related to capacity, the clearer it would seem to be that the tax power and not the police power is being invoked.

Identification of the tax power as the basis of social security legislation should, however, have brought with it awareness that this power was being used as a factor of control in the process of distribution—that it was being used as a means of securing the needs of non-wage-earners in a wage economy. Actually, however, the strength of tradition, and especially the failure and unwillingness to conceive the tax power as other than a method of meeting the necessary expenses of government, has resulted in perpetuating the view that the beneficiaries of public assistance are wards of the government and should be aided only if "worthy" of the sacrifices of others in

69

their behalf. To be eligible, in other words, they must be something more than non-employable members of our society.

To be sure, an individual must always perform the conditions laid down for the exercise of a right, but laying down, as a condition to the exercise of his economic security rights, that the individual must be "good" or "worthy" and must not violate the conventions or mores of the community, singles him out as an individual who cannot, like his fellows, do what he pleases so long as he does not behave in a way that society has found it expedient to interdict. Such a condition deprives him of rights regarded as essential to the maintenance of a free society, removes from him the sacred privilege of self-determination, violates basic tenets of our system of criminal law, and in fact prostitutes the law itself.

The modes of human behavior are devious, defying classification, but the category of punishable crimes is disproportionately brief. And even in its prescribed reach, the rules of common law exhibit beyond all else the efforts of mankind to preserve for the individual every safeguard of freedom compatible with the social order. When you hear it argued that a public assistance recipient should not be allowed to live in a manner that injures his health lest he become a still greater expense to the public, consider how many people there are whose earning power alone sustains them and yet who persistently live in a manner to injure their health and do thereby threaten and in due course heavily burden the public purse.

There is a delightful subtlety in the question sung by Gilbert and Sullivan: " 'Is it weakness of intellect, Birdie,' I cried, 'or a rather tough worm in your little inside?' " Because security is a prime necessity in the life of every individual, for the sake of which most individuals will sacrifice all else, insecurity is an evil, independent of its cause in the particular case. Therefore it is as inconsistent to condition assistance or security upon personal adequacy, whether of mind or body or of attitude or of behavior, as it is to condition it upon tax payments. You cannot, of course, condition assistance upon behavior and still use it as an instrumentality to bolster the individual's freedom of action and feeling of independence.

You cannot, of course, buy morality or good behavior. The behavior that it would condemn, society must assume responsibility for outlawing. To the extent that it has enacted criminal laws it must assume responsibility for their enforcement in such manner as to preserve basic freedoms of the individual. It follows that the failure of society to recognize its ethical obligations to the individual constitutes an insidious threat to our basic freedoms.

Since the Supreme Court of the United States rested the Social Security Act squarely on the tax power, rather than the police power, the legal-right point of view has steadily gained acceptance. Thus, case by case, we may ultimately succeed in incorporating the common needs of human beings into the pattern of our system of legal rights and obligations. We shall ultimately find the relations of individuals with society stated in legal terms. But law always has constituted and always will constitute a mirror of society and will reflect throughout its pages the philosophy by which we live. So until we stop trying to strengthen the human will by suppressing it, we will still see human welfare entrusted to the unloving arms of the police power.

All prejudice is subtle, but there is nothing quite so subtle or so elusive as that which seeks to justify the withholding of social and economic prerogatives on the grounds of an inferior moral sense. Some lines in Wordsworth's *The Excursion* (Book IX) may be recalled on this point:

> Gifts nobler are vouchsafed alike to all;
> Reason, and, with that reason, smiles and tears;
> Imagination, freedom in the will;
> Conscience to guide and check; and death to be

Foretasted, . .
Strange, then, .
. . . if the Almighty, to this point
Liberal and undistinguishing, should hide
The excellence of moral qualities
From common understanding; leaving truth
And virtue, difficult, abstruse, and dark;
Hard to be won, and only by a few;

        .   .   .   .   .   .

. . . . Believe it not:
The primal duties shine aloft—like stars;

        .   .   .   .   .   .

The generous inclination, the just rule,
Kind wishes, and good actions, and pure thoughts—
No mystery is here! Here is no boon
For high—yet not for low; for proudly graced—
Yet not for meek of heart. The smoke ascends
To heaven as lightly from the cottage hearth
As from the haughtiest palace. He, whose soul
Ponders this true equality, may walk
The fields of earth with gratitude and hope;

        .   .   .   .   .   .

JOINT ACTION AND THE SENSE OF RESPONSIBILITY

If you would develop a sense of responsibility in individuals, you would do well to put them in situations which they fully dominate and the outcome of which thus depends entirely on the decisions they themselves make. This is a significant truth which seems to me to give the lie to a great deal that is commonly said about the efficacy of competition. Competition may sharpen wits but it does not create character. It is not the struggle against odds but awareness that the consequences are of one's own making that creates character. Hence it is that the legal right to command action initiates awareness of responsibility for the action that results. Just as men derive a prideful sense of independence from the legal rights they possess, so also an awareness of responsibility springs from one's prerogatives and legal status.

With these principles in mind consider, too, that other legend—that the public servicing of man's needs fosters his irresponsibility. What seems to be meant is that the individual's sense of responsibility for his own welfare, his self-reliance, is lessened or destroyed.

We must, of course, frankly recognize that the processes by which human security and freedom are promoted in society inevitably involve some pooling of the products of our utterly different capacities and resources. To make the process effective, however, there must be reserved to each individual the legally effective right to such use of these products as is necessary to meet his needs as determined in the application of a legislated standard. Community or governmental action never destroys the sense of independence and responsibility of those whose participation in the service or benefit is derived from the accepted laws of the community.

For example, one of the chief needs of a man and his family is the education and training of his children. It so happens that parents often lack the kind of education and the kind of skills their children need. They also lack the ability to teach others what they themselves know. So families join together and through community action provide a more effective and diversified training for their children. This involves a transfer of the individual's allegiance from direct and personal effort to the communal undertaking. The need for education and training is universal. If the project succeeds, an educational pool will be created from which individuals may draw directly. The result is an actual substitution of a social agency for individual action. The school hot lunch program often began in just this fashion. Parents got together and staffed the service through a system of alternating assignments and, of course, pooled their resources to make necessary purchases.

The entry upon such a joint undertaking poses a serious problem for the individual, because it requires a pledge of allegiance and the devotion to it of a portion of the individual's time and labor and material resources, all of which he might otherwise have used himself in his own attempt to meet the needs of himself and his family. He must determine, therefore, whether the cooperative venture will satisfy the need and achieve the aim better than he himself could achieve it alone.

This process involves no sacrifice of the original aim. The potentialities of this kind of socialization do not seem to be limited by any obvious economic or cultural consideration. In other words, what applies here to individual and family cooperation, applies as well to action on a community—or state-wide basis. There is no sound reason why we should not transfer our allegiance to efforts conceived on a broader and broader basis, provided we may thus more effectively achieve the security and freedom we seek. Our aims will not be prejudiced. They may be more effectively attained, provided we are individually assured of a legal right to what we need. We thus retain a sense of having maintained our individual responsibilities.

The security process thus involves pledging our allegiance and our material efforts to our construction of a common stock-pile capable of attaining our security aims more effectively and efficiently than we can achieve them individually. Methods that do this will command the transfer of our allegiance. The essential condition to this efficacy is the assurance of a legal right to what we need from the common pool.

Once established, such a pattern can have no effect to destroy individual initiative. It simply redirects initiative into a more significant and socially meaningful objective. Once the pattern is established, it becomes the milieu of life, a way of

74

life itself, to which the individual adjusts his own life. It becomes nothing more than a medium which life uses for its own purposes.

Take the American Union. It began with mere articles of confederation. Read these articles once again and see how important to its drafters was the territorial integrity of the particular state's domain. But the integrity of the state's domain became of less and less moment as the Union's domain took on a greater significance to its residents. It is that way with all cooperative enterprise.

We greatly fear the discouragement of competition. To justify this attitude we stress the natural competitive urge. I heard this well illustrated by the story of what occurred in a regiment during the night after the soldiers were paid. It happened that there was no commercial outlet for the deluge of coin that fell among the men; so they took to gambling, mainly "crap" games. In the morning two or three men had all the money, and the speaker's point was that this eventuality was not only normal, but inevitable. But the speaker's conclusion that it is folly to strive for a more balanced economy and individual security does not follow, even though it be granted that the aim of actual equality, economically speaking, is far distant and perhaps not even justifiable. For if the competitive spirit, in the sense of getting ahead of the other fellow, is so natural and inevitable in its effects, why fear efforts to sublimate or make a more constructive use of such an impulse?

Life reaches higher planes through a sublimation or redirection of its competitive instincts. The spirit of competition is never so exhilarating as when it is expressed in the effort of the individual or group to hold up his own end of a common endeavor, to contribute more than others to a joint undertaking. There is no loss of freedom or opportunity in joint enterprise. The competition between individuals becomes a competition in efficiency and in the excellence of performance.

The competitive spirit is sublimated, given an outlet that is socially desirable, but its values are not sacrificed.

So it is with the economic security of the human race. It involves a recognition of the fact that we are all members of a society. The economic might of that society should become responsive to the needs of its individual members, to meet the common needs of human life, and, I would add, to the extent that it is possible to enrich individual life. In this way the individual in society can be made conscious of a strength that is not of himself alone but of the composite strength of all life.

If you argue that this will destroy initiative you merely deny the ability of the individual to cooperate successfully in the achievement of his objectives. Competition is conditioned on the retention of rights but not on the retention of rights denied to others. We need the stimulus of achievement but not the stimulus of victory over our fellow men. In the long run, the ends of life will not be achieved through the competition of wills, for the victory in such a competition is the submergence of the defeated will. Society depends on the ability of mankind to achieve a satisfactory adjustment between the several paths followed by the wills of men in the pursuit of their objectives. Life is always striving to reach its objectives, and the social process is a method to that end. We should measure our achievements in terms of the significance of individual life and character, a significance not measured in terms of the relative insignificance of our fellows when compared to ourselves but in terms of a society in which the security, freedom, and greatness of one individual becomes compatible with that of every other. That compatibility is achieved by law, for it is law that makes the independence of each of us compatible with the interdependence of all of us.

Chapter 6

LAW AS A SOURCE OF NOTIONS OF FREEDOM

W E HAVE BEEN dealing up to this point with the system of legal rights essential to preserve the natural and highly developed sense of prerogative on the part of the individual in the context of our existing economic pattern. We have endeavored to show the need to extend the legal system in terms of the individual as a means of preserving his freedom of will, to give scope and play to his instinct for self-determination, and to foster his own sense of moral responsibility.

Now let us think in somewhat broader terms of society, of what law and the system of individual legal rights and obligations so extended mean in terms of an ideally self-operative, self-administered, and free society. For this purpose we need to go back and see what the true meaning and function of law is, not in terms of authority, which is so commonly mistaken for law, but in terms of the rule of law in the ideal sense as a guide and challenge to the human will.

The best example of how law, in the ideal sense, works, how it evokes the sense of freedom and stimulates the individual is the survey of a game. Have you ever asked yourself why the participation in a game is so excellent a medium for self-expression and character development? This question is

77

often superficially answered in terms of the rein given to the competitive instincts of the individual and his "zest" for conquest. But have you ever considered that here, in a game, and perhaps here alone, we human beings really do act almost completely under the aegis of law? That, rather than competition, is the real source of the game's restorative value for the human spirit. Analyze the process step by step and you must be convinced that this is the truth.

Your first step upon entering a game is the assumption of a distinct personality. You become clothed in a personality defined by the rules of the game. You assume a legal or game personality. You may describe yourself as a first baseman, as a right guard, or as a dealer. But however you describe yourself you will see that what you have described is a legal status —one of the focal points in a legal pattern with rights and obligations suitable to the position. These rights and duties are defined by the rules under whose empery you have thus put both yourself and all others with whom you have dealings. Your status, your rights, your obligations, all are secure, for the rules of the game are almost sure to be followed. The game indeed is defined by its rules. These are purely abstract. They are wholly free of will and dictation. They are pure rules of action composed usually in some physical setting which they serve to interpret and fashion till it becomes an arena of human action, just as, for example, the rules of the highway, in relation to the highway pattern itself, provide individuals with an arena on which they can operate successfully. Now the rules of the game have many functions. They, in fact, define the very goals that the players seek. One wins only in the context of the rules of the game. They determine inexorably the consequences of the player's action, every play that he makes. He acts solely in relation to the rules. Their empery is accepted like a fact or a circumstance. Finally, they challenge and stimulate him for he uses the rules to win. The

78

game is otherwise unmanaged. An umpire or a referee is but an interpreter of the rules. He *can* be wrong. Such is the conception. This, then, may furnish an introduction to the real function of law in society.

Law gave birth to the concept of freedom. True it is that you can have no security in a situation in which every person and everything around you acts capriciously, unpredictably, or, in other words, lawlessly; but the point I wish to make is that while you would have no security in such an environment, it is more significant that you would have no freedom in such an environment. The reason you could not be free in such a situation is that you could not get anywhere you wanted to go or successfully do anything you wanted to do. You could make no plan in the expectation of carrying it out. You cannot possibly carry out any aim or goal of your own unless you have some basis for calculating what results may follow from any given act or activity of your own. Unless you can determine in advance what are the prospects and limitations of a given course of behavior, you cannot act intelligently. Whatever intelligence you may have will do you no good. You cannot adjust your own step to anyone else's step nor can you relate your conduct to any series of events or occurrences outside yourself except to the extent that they follow a pattern that you can learn about in advance of your action.

Now there is one possible situation in which act and rule—will and law—merge. That situation is one in which both the act, and the pattern in which the act takes place, are decreed by the same mind. The human race, for example, has conceived of a Supreme Being whom they call God, and having conceived of him as possessing infinite capacity, it seems at first thought to make little difference whether we ascribe an event to His will or to His law. Thus you often hear it said, "It is the will of God," or, "It is the law of God," without differentiating between these two things. Everything is thus conceived as ordained by God, whether by prearrangement or upon the spur of the moment. Actually, in failing to differentiate, you deny the existence of law and ascribe everything to will.

Of course, our human society cannot operate that way, for we do not have an all-embracing mind to administer it. If we did, we would deny any freedom whatsoever to the individuals in our society, because society is composed of people and all people have wills and these wills constitute the very pattern which this supreme dictator would need to control in order to produce order without law. Neither, of course, is there any ultimate freedom in man if his acts, as well as the world in which he acts, are directed by Deity. If there be no pre-established rules, there can be no freedom.

The only way to promote freedom is to devise a set of rules and thus construct a pattern which the various members of that society can follow. Each can then determine his own acts in the light of his knowledge of the rules. On this basis each can predict his field of action in advance and what results are likely to ensue from his acts; and so he gains freedom to plan and to carry out his plans. The more you attempt to administer society, however, the less free it becomes. There is opportunity for freedom of choice only in acting subject to the rules, and then only if the rules are freed of any element of will or dictation. If these rules are just rules that tell you what method or act will yield what results, like the rules of a game, you can then freely determine your own play. You can use the rules to win the game. The more abstract and objective the rule, the freer is the individual in the choice of his alternatives. The rules must be so written as to cover every possible eventuality of choice and action.

Freedom implies the ability to act at will while the pattern in relation to which you act remains fixed. One needs, therefore, a predetermined pattern in relation to which he may act.

The establishment of this pattern, and whatever adds to this pattern, is an act of creation. It was the form and order of things that God created. To challenge life and its will God seems to have employed His will in creating or establishing a universe that is to be comprehended by its laws. Man thus found his inspiration in a law-abiding world. Only when you can act in a pattern that is void of wilful interference can you have assurance of freedom.

We have all at one time or another sought to create something—be it a mere idea, a paragraph, a mechanical toy, something artistic, or a garden. We have then experienced the pleasure of standing back when it is finished and saying "See what I have made. See, it works—it has meaning, it has influence." In the Book of Genesis this attitude is ascribed to the Creator Himself. At each stage in the process of creation he is said to have stood back, looked at what he had made, and said that it was good. Now what is it that makes it good, be it great or small, a tiny garden or all creation? Is it not the fact that this created something has been given an independent existence, that it has become something for itself? It tells a story. It has significance or capacity in and of itself. Even if this thing you have produced requires your continued action or attention, you would nevertheless point to what it will do when your hand leaves off. The interesting fact is that it carries on, and so demonstrates its capacities. And if it be a living thing your pride would expand with its capacity for growth and development, its ability to lay its hand upon the world outside itself and adapt what it finds there to its own uses, to realize and express itself and to achieve.

We can look at all creation in this light, see how it works, study the principles of its operation. And to me at least it would greatly detract from the joy and charm of the picture if this creation did not appear to be self-operating, if it did not appear relatively autonomous, automatic and self-actuating.

The whole point is missed if what one observes is a purely passive submission to an external actuating agency. I noticed, for example, the other day a mechanical bird fastened to the side of a glass filled with liquid and this bird continued slowly but constantly to drop its head to the liquid and back again and nothing actuated it but the nature of the liquid itself. It was almost perpetual motion. In this lay its interest.

Society and all human relationships must operate on their own, so to speak. The principles of adjustment must work automatically. Unless a rule is at least ninety per cent effective without the intervention of what we are pleased to call law enforcement, it does not deserve the name of law. There is the same need for a law-observant society as there is for an order of nature.

Now I suspect that if you are having difficulty with my interpretation of law up to this point it is because you are thinking in terms of the mixture of will and law that to a great extent passes for law in our society. You are thus confusing the conception of law with the conception of authority. You are thinking of law in relation to human beings as a system of controls upon their action which dictates their choice of alternatives. This is will, not law, and only to the extent that these controls are not rigidly maintained, and only in their relaxation, is there freedom.

But if law is properly defined in terms of a rule that defines the consequences of action and does this inexorably but does no more, then the will of man would be quite as free under man's regime as under God's—and this while the rules of the game are in full operation. To be sure, other people may not act in relation to the rules so as to make it possible for you to lay out your own course reliably; but if they do, and to the extent that they do, you become free.

Thus, the widely accepted rule that motor vehicles should pass one another on the same side (be it right or left) is a purely abstract guide, yet it gives their operators, at one and the same time, both security and freedom in reaching their divergent goals. The rule itself embraces no element of authority or of will or compulsion. It merely says that that is a good way to reach one another's aims successfully. As a sound rule it is *in no sense restrictive*. The absence of such a rule would leave you greatly restricted. It might even stop you from going at all. The sounder the rule, the more freedom it gives you.

Thus to the extent that we develop sound, efficacious rules we develop law but at the same time we are eliminating the need for authority and policing. Take the highway. To the extent that we can devise rules that comprehend every possibility, and to the extent that we can establish a pattern in which the highway, as physically constructed, precisely relates itself to these rules, we present the driver with an established pattern all of which is law. The analogy to a game is here freely borne out; for the rules of a game are similarly related to the physical pattern to which they give meaning and expression and which they interpret. The more serviceable the highway pattern, the less need for any impact of will upon the driver, that is to say, of any policing. The ultimate reason why this is so is that in all you have done you have extended the freedom of the driver. You have not circumscribed it. You have extended it. The driver now has a more comprehensive frame of reference, the achievement of which steadily lessens the urge to capricious action. The ultimate objective is to bring about a situation in which the driver finds *that he can do nothing more advantageous to himself and to his ends than to make the best adjustment* that it is possible to make to this established pattern. The ultimate challenge to life will then lie in the extent to which he may succeed in achieving that adjustment. The pattern of the highway may not be as complex as is the universe itself which God has devised for man to walk

83

in, but in the course of its development and in the effort to adapt itself to every eventuality, it will tend always to constitute a more and more complete, precise and better adjusted instrumentality for man's use.

You will find the very opposite situation in *Alice in Wonderland*. Alice, you will recall, found it well-nigh impossible to adjust herself to a world thus come alive in the form of unruly wills, presided over by a queen who personifies the executive unguided by law.

The Queen, you remember, was an unmitigated executive. If to some she seems emotional, the effect must be ascribed to the abysses of her contempt for judicial procedure. Her decrees yielded to no argument—except, of course, when without due inquiry into the circumstances, she tried to apply her rigid format, "Off with his head," to the Cheshire Cat. Even at this point the King supported her. He showed convincingly that whatever had a head could be beheaded. That's the crown lawyer for you. "I don't think they play at all fairly," Alice complained, "and they all quarrel so dreadfully one can't hear one's-self speak—and they don't seem to have any rules in particular: at least, if there are, nobody attends to them." Alice was still thinking in procedural terms. However, Alice was also concerned about the instability of the frame of reference. "...and you've no idea," she went on, "how confusing it is all the things being alive: for instance, there's the arch I've got to go through next walking about at the other end of the ground—and I should have croqueted the Queen's hedgehog just now, only it ran away when it saw mine coming!" You see, Alice believed that issues should be frankly met. However, as Alice concluded, "The Queen is so extremely—likely to win, that it's hardly worth while finishing the game."

This is a bad dream, but it is a dream that is reflected in some degree in the waking minds of many individuals today, individuals who see themselves as living from hour to hour under the whip-hand of authority. Day and night, in most of what he listens to or reads, law is represented to the individual as a superior will directing his acts and decisions. I fear that our children are growing up to regard law as a system of mandates or edicts to be obeyed or, if possible, outwitted or defied. A child may thus lose the sense of personal accountability, and the awareness of his personal responsibility. Worse than this he may develop a feeling of frustration and the sense of being continually driven to act against his will rather than under its controls. He is finding himself dependent for life, not on a subservient, responsive environment, but upon an environment which reserves to itself the prerogative of passing judgment on every step he takes or contemplates. Its pronouncements are categorical—whether yes or no. This will-minded environment breeds a rebellious and a hopeless spirit.

During the course of one day I heard over the radio not less than five references to law in terms of obedience. Each one of the speakers conceived of law as a dictation of alternatives in human behavior. In fact, this idea seemed to be for all of these speakers the primary significance of the impact of "law" on human life. Possibly they had a more realistic conception of the existing situation than I did, but by the end of the day I had personally conceived a firm desire to go out and break some law, to do a few things of my own choosing, regardless of some legal prohibition.

I knew a child once who, being possessed of some spirit, threw himself against the paneling of a heavy oak door, screaming as he beat his head against the door, "Go ahead and lick me, I want you to lick me!" Now other children may exhibit less outward spirit and the situations that confront them may be less outwardly dramatic, but the urge within them may be all the greater for its suppression. I am sure that there is no more effective method of producing lawlessness than rigid rules that dictate behavior and leave the individual with less opportunity to pursue alternatives of his own devising. Can we never see that sound laws and abstract rules create alternatives? Can we not see in law a challenge to the imaginative conceptions of man's mind and will?

It is suggested to me that it is the method of authoritarianism, the rigid invocation of authority, yielding no alternatives, that creates harmful effects and bad traits of character. But note this phrase, "yielding no alternatives." Alternatives exist for the individual only to the extent that his own will (or choice) is free in terms of his willingness to accept a variety of different consequences inherent in the rules of the game. We are talking in terms of action, in dynamic terms. In these terms authority (that is, a command upon the individual) is by its very definition a limitation or dictation of his choice and involves the requirement that he accept one set of consequences rather than another.

I think there is a great deal of confusion between authority —the use of authority, the force of authority—and law in modern psychology. There can be no doubt, I think, that the psychologists are right in tracing many of man's ills to the element of authoritarianism in his environment; but this authoritative element is significant to the extent that it is wilful and capricious rather than merely declaratory of the rules and principles by which we ought to be guided in making up our own minds. The will that requires action in one direction rather than in another is not law. It is the other half of the law and will dichotomy.

Obviously, to act from hour to hour under the leash of external directives and commands, especially unreasoned directives and commands, will breed immaturity in human beings. But the rule of law itself and the authority, be it executive or judicial, which compels one to accept the consequences that law decrees, are two very different things; and I am disturbed at the lack of recognition accorded to the fact that adherence to law was the most significant characteristic of the environment in which the human race matured. The essential reason is that man's physical environment has allowed him to make his own decisions while compelling him to accept their consequences. Nature proves that action under law, inexorable law, develops maturity, not immaturity.

There is a failure to recognize the significance of the fact that law's purpose is to make authority and force unnecessary in our environment. If this were not generally true our wills would be at once defeated by the counter forces set in motion by any activity of our own. Man's will cannot stand up for a moment, or maintain its integrity, in an environment that is wilfully opposed to it. A physical law states that action and re-action are always equal but this is true only where law reigns. It is not true of the will. Wilful opposition knows no such limitations. This thought must embarrass anyone who hears the external world described as a great "external will." Man's total environment, past, present, and future, has sometimes been regarded as a vast external authority, compelling in its impact, to which man must in all things submit. Indeed all law has been conceived by some writers as a part of this great external will or authority. Such a conception denies to man's environment the most elemental prerequisites to the development of individuality.

The laws of man differ from the laws of nature; but the fundamental attributes of law are of universal significance. There is, for example, an ethic of sorts in all law, since the need for a principle or rule of action arises whenever there is more than one moving object in the same area. The individual objective and movement of one object needs consideration from the other. Adjustment between the two therefore becomes necessary, and both must observe whatever abstract rule of action will permit both to achieve their ends without conflict. The great difference between human law and physical law is this—

that man-made laws address themselves to life and are designed, therefore, to promote adjustment between living interests. The action that they must harmonize is voluntary—that is, willed action. Consequently, on the part of either, the will to harmonize is necessary. The result is that man-made law must be written as an appeal to the human will. The system becomes a system of rules for the guidance of human wills. The cultivation of a will ethically motivated and responsive to law is an undertaking of a spiritual nature.

When man-made rules seek to by-pass the will and address themselves to the action of the individual they lose the character of law. They become commands, orders, or edicts, which is to say that they become other wills. As wills, they address themselves directly to the mechanisms of action. In fact, they resent the intervention of the individual's own will. They will brook no intervening mind.

It follows that all ethical action is by its very nature voluntary action, that is, willed by the individual himself.

It was said recently that human beings should be guided by their good sense and simply behave rationally and sensibly. The speaker deplored the effect of the sense of guilt on the human personality, but if I understood him correctly, he urged that the evil effects he complained of were the inevitable effects of the very existence of objectively framed ethical standards, especially, I believe, those drafted and promulgated by human societies.

The answer to this kind of thinking is that ethics and ethical standards came into being with the will itself. Here is a man, driving along the highway, who suddenly finds that he must either strike a pedestrian or hit a tree. In the latter event he will probably kill himself. What does the rule of good sense prescribe in this situation? What is sensible behavior in a world into which moral law has come? Is it sensible, or is it crazy, may I ask, to act in a way that is contrary to your own

88

interests in order to avoid injuring another? You say, "That depends on your standards," do you not?

I doubt that there is anything injurious to human personality in the sense of guilt, in penitence, or even in remorse. The Hebrew nation was law-conscious. There is, perhaps, a corresponding emphasis in their thinking upon penitence, but this is a normal, rational, and healthy reaction. What hurts is the failure and inability to correct or alleviate the consequences of one's wrong decisions, especially those that hurt other people, while conscience presses for action. The effect of this struggle is like that of an engine running with open throttle while the brakes are firmly set. There you have destructive conflict, frustration. A lawyer will recognize this effect when the superior will of the community is brought to bear upon individuals to compel them to act or take a position that betrays their moral sense or their mental integrity. While their conscience drives them on, the judgments of an undisciplined society forcibly restrain them. The individual will is crushed, and the world applauds. Every occasion in which individuals choose to suffer the sanction, rather than to obey a rule that violates their principles, proves the case for a sound and protective judicial procedure. False codes must be challenged, but they will be challenged in normal course only by individuals made secure and free by law. Martyrdom is the ultimate test of the will.

Legal science has used every promising means of avoiding man's subjection to human judgments and discretion. The judicial process was invented as a means of dealing scientifically and objectively with situations when individually conceived patterns are out of adjustment with the society's legal pattern. The process was made as objective and circumstantial, as possible, in the effort not to subject one individual to the whims and caprices, or the views and predilections of others. The latter half of the guaranties contained in the Bill of

Rights, and most rules of judicial procedure, were conceived for this purpose. Those who do away with the rule of *stare decisis*, that is to say, of following legal precedent, must also make their peace with this principle, because it is a device that limits the occasion for individual predilection and improvisation. Law recognizes that it is not good that man's acts should be directed by a will not his own. If you bring a legal action against another and win, about all you get is money damages. The law has always hesitated to command men to act. It prefers to let man act as he wills and make him take the consequences, that is, pay the piper. This nature ever does. It is the way law acts, and to the extent that the consequences imposed upon the doer are circumstantially related to what he did—that is, constitute the normal or natural result of one's actions—the result seems sound.

The cause of religion is impeded by this same confusion between will and law. It engenders attitudes that are ill content to abide the event of man's inner struggle with himself and concentrates on man's acts rather than on his spirit. God is properly described as both the Creator and the Preserver of the universe. By His will He creates it and He establishes it under law, which means that He creates it as a continuing self-operative, autonomous process. In so doing He gives to man the power to participate in the creative process as a delegatee of the responsible will of God Himself. Man thus becomes aware of his accountability as a part of the eternal intelligence that is ultimately responsible for all things.

But it is in the organization of society we call government that the issue bears most heavily on the affairs of men. Have you not noticed that back of every jurisdictional contest, back, for example, of the contest that is waged between the respective protagonists of state rights and federal prerogatives in America, back of the emotional feeling that is engendered between the different departments of government, especially between the legislature and executive agencies, back of the whole debate over the establishment of a legally effective world order, a world government, lies the blatant assumption that the words "government" and "authority" are synonyms. Government officials, especially those engaged in effectuating the law, or must I say "enforcing the law," are "the authorities." The whole issue in the minds of those who debate these matters hangs on the conception that power and prerogative are at stake in each case. The issue is conceived in terms of superior will. The fact that the issue is so conceived tends to maintain the old regime in each case and to retard the advent of a more democratic method. This is true, for example, of the relation between the several states and the Federal Government which is coming to concern itself with every phase of governmental activity. As originally conceived the relationship between the states and the federal government was largely set out and dealt with in legal terms. But it has become in many instances an administrative and hence supervisory relationship.

Again the attitude of the Congress toward the executive departments is motivated largely by the conviction that these government agencies and officials are authoritative and willminded. Some legislators think it quite unrealistic to suppose that the executive departments will adhere to the limitations and proscriptions of the statutes and the statutorily defined programs they administer. It is supposed that the withholding of money is the only effective control the Congress has. The truth is that most administrators welcome a law that, by its own terms, carefully prescribes the conditions and limitations of its application.

In the same way, the hesitancy to seek a political jurisdiction of wider scope, in which the ultimate autonomy of existing sovereignties would be merged, is born of the same conception of government in either case as an authoritative controller of one's destiny. Actually, of course, even under existing conditions the broader the ultimate jurisdiction, the less concerned it is with local policing and with constraint upon will. Like a high court of law, its benignity is the greater because of its preoccupation with the highest legal conceptions that we have achieved.

Just suppose you did not think of government as a directive authority. Suppose you thought of it as an agency whose primary concern was to conceive and draft wise laws that, being followed, would give the individual and his community a freedom, a protected freedom of choice and action they had never before known; to provide security of life on a surer basis than had been previously conceived; to see to it through the wisdom of its laws, as well as through judicial means, that neither strength nor shrewdness could outwit these laws; and by all these means to reduce the police power and policing to a minimum never before possible—well, what harm would there be in it?

Chapter 7

LAW IN SOCIAL CONSTRUCTION AND RECONSTRUCTION

LET US GLANCE for a moment at the historical development of our search for law and legal prerogative and see if we can determine what has occurred in recent times to prejudice this development. For there are many signs and omens of recidivism in the development of human character and significant personality.

Sir Henry Maine originated the phrase "from status to contract" in describing the processes by which the individual acquired a legal personality and legal rights and obligations. The word "status," used in relation to the individual's position in the ancient family and clan, indicated the general fact that his privileges and responsibilities were mere incidents of his family relationship and were accorded only in token of his allegiance to the clan's head or chieftain. The feudal system was in many respects a harking back to this primary security system.

The gradual acquisition of a legal personality by the individual can be expressed, however, in the broader terms of a progression from the directive will of a chieftain to the development of an objective system of rules of behavior as the principal means of creating a human society and of expressing the

93

social, or shall we say legal, significance of the individual in society. We have thus sought to create a society ruled by law. We would thus project man's legally ruled natural environment into the social order. Primitive men in their relationships with one another recognized no law in the sense of ethical rules of action for the adjustment of their relationships. Tribal chiefs issued their commands, the so-called themistes. These commands ruled only the specific case. They laid down no pattern of law or "nomos" on the basis of which a human society could function automatically. Even Plato and Aristotle recognized no basic substratum of law by which they might have tested the legitimacy of a ruler's or government's directives.

The significance of Rome lies in her recognition of the fact that the building of human society is man's job and that his success requires recourse to the methods of nature. Rome made it her paramount aim to establish a reliable pattern of behavior throughout society for the purpose of avoiding conflict, of adjusting human relationships, and of protecting the interests of the individual. Rome was thus intent upon introducing some of nature's order into the social fabric. The real god of Rome was law. Greece had been intent upon exemplifying the significance of human personality and individuality. Her conception of the potentialities of manhood was symbolized in the supporting columns that sustained her architectural triumphs and in her statuary. It was the purpose of Rome to conserve this basic strength and to provide a medium for the preservation and development of individuality through the construction of a basic system of legal rights and obligations descriptive of human relationships. She thus set about weaving the strands of the social pattern. There is a close analogy between the ordering of these human relationships and the construction of a system of roads throughout the Empire. The purpose of both was to make security and freedom compatible with one another.

When the law-making and law-administering agencies of Rome fell, human society became in common parlance a free-for-all. There followed a genuine scramble for security as the first essential of life. This scramble for security ultimately resolved itself into the feudal system. The main idea of the feudal system was to give the individual protection from others in return for his allegiance to oneself. This allegiance was not to law, it should be noted, but to the will of an adopted champion. The prerogatives of the individual found no sanction save in the physical strength of a guardian knight. Feudal relationships were not legal relationships; they were authoritative and supervisory. They resembled guardian-ward relationships or in the broader sense parent-child relationships. Under these circumstances human beings lost their own rights of self-determination and self-management. They obtained for themselves an institutional status in a chieftain's household as did the members of the ancient clan or tribe. The security of the whole establishment rested, just as did the security of the primitive family, in the fact of its isolation and in the impregnability of its defenses. The dignity of men and the sanctity of women were alike sacrificed to the whims of an earthly lord. There is no price too dear for security.

But man's need of a legal environment for the preservation of his developing individuality was a normal instinct, developed through the long ages of his natural existence. The absolute administrator, King John, was at length confronted with this demand. The only pattern of law available at the time lay in the customs of the fiefs themselves. Here at least was some substitute or reprieve for the reign of will. Magna Carta thus represented the reaffirmation of the principle that an enduring society can be constructed only on legal foundations.

95

At the dawn of the eighteenth century, however, the feudal bargain had lost all semblance of mutuality. There survived only claims of inherited right and privilege that were founded originally on the promise of protection. But as knighthood had turned into aristocracy, so had its protégés descended to the rank of abject and cowering human forms, from whom the long reign of will had removed the very substance of personality and self-assurance. This reign of will, except in those few instances in which isolated human beings had found strength to defy it, was fast destroying the individuality that earlier generations in a healthier environment had throughout the ages been building up. Only in Great Britain had the rule of law been successfully promoted. Comparing the two situations Montesquieu saw that the freedom of individuals could perhaps be safeguarded in an organized society if the government was so ordered that it would not become a law unto itself. In other words, the ultimate authority must be law and not will. His findings were summarized by John Adams in the famous phrase which he wrote into the Constitution of the State of Massachusetts, "to the end that there shall be a government of laws and not of men."

Thus Montesquieu gave a practical turn to the "return to nature" movement of the continental philosophers. He showed that you could provide for mankind in a social setting some of the stability of man's natural environment through the substitution of law for will in the establishment of social institutions. In this way it was possible to save human beings from the whims and caprices of other men and from the destruction of character that may result from man's attempt to rule his fellow man. The need to provide a scope for the individual's self-expression, and to increase man's awareness of himself and his faith in himself and his potentialities, led at once to the formalized declaration of human rights.

"We hold these truths to be self-evident," runs the Declaration of Independence, "that all men are created equal, that they are endowed by their Creator with certain unalienable rights, that among these are life, liberty and the pursuit of happiness. That to secure these rights, governments are instituted among men. . . ." The Declaration of Independence was one of the first, if not the first, expression in an important official document of the kind of thinking that kindled the French Revolution. Our own Bill of Rights, the French Declaration of Rights, and a great many constitutional provisions of similar import followed.

Many writers have sought to elicit the deeper meaning behind the eighteenth century's great outburst against existing social institutions. What was said during these momentous days is quite as important as what was done. The deepest human instincts were asserting themselves. Human beings throughout the whole of our western culture had become aware that existing social and political institutions were doing more harm than good to the development of human life on earth. The upper crust of society had hardened and crystallized over the struggling life beneath it. Individual life was bound down, hamstrung, and frustrated. For about the first time in history there was a very genuine widespread fear and some understanding of the harm that human society might do to human life.

What we need today, from this standpoint, is a bill of positive or affirmative human rights sufficient to guarantee the independence of the individual in our modern interdependent human society. The essential justification for this affirmative construction and implementation of Jefferson's "unalienable right" to life is usually referred to as the industrial revolution. The fact of key importance is that some eighty per cent or more of the population, at least in industrialized countries, have come to live in reliance upon their ability to participate

97

in the operations of the organizations and agencies by which human life is now implemented and supported. This dependency would normally be reflected in any modern bill of rights—such as that composed under the auspices of the United Nations.[1]

In an article in a law review I have stated the issue as follows:

> ... the fundamental developments which have resulted in interposing the whole social and economic structure between the individual and his ultimate resources in nature must be recognized as having deprived the individual, or as having at best made him a third party obligee, of nature's underlying commitment. Nature has maintained individual life from a time when the individual had substantially no capacity of his own. We cannot achieve the similar security of the individual at the hands of society without suitable substitution for that commitment in terms of human law. A guaranty of the opportunity to earn a living, even if it is given, will meet about half the problem. Less than half the race has normally any substantial earning capacity at a particular moment of time." [2]

Two kinds of legal rights are needed to provide basic security for the individual in society. In the first group are things essential to the maintenance of life—for those in the labor market, a job and wage insurance—for others, food, shelter, and clothes —for all individuals remedial health services. Since human beings are physically, apart from sex, practically identical in their organic structure, the needs of individuals are likewise identical and so their resources may be most effectively pooled for their common use. But in their capacities, fortunately, they vary to an infinite degree. Hence, by the word "job," we of necessity refer to the opportunity to participate in the orga-

1. See Universal Declaration of Human Rights, Art. 25(1).
2. "Public Assistance as a Social Obligation," *Harvard Law Review*, vol. 63, no. 2, p. 271.

nized work of the world in ways that enlist the individual's highest capacities.

As the technique of organization develops, as the various functions of mankind become more and more highly organized, the basis on which individuals may be included or excluded from participation in any enterprise becomes increasingly significant. The individual's right to participate becomes, therefore, more and more a matter for legal cognizance—a matter for the law and for the courts. The individual can no longer be left at the mercy of whim and caprice in matters vital to his security in a closely organized society. That is why discriminatory practices in terms of individual characteristics, whether of color, creed, sex, or nationality are becoming so productive of social tensions. The individual often finds himself between the Scylla and Charybdis of obligation and prejudice. It is an extraordinary fact that while the individual today is generally held personally responsible for developing an employment relationship, the legislatures of the country question their own ability to guarantee him an opportunity of employment. There is a question whether they may properly expect the individual to assume personal responsibility for developing opportunities that they feel quite incapable of assuring him.

The second basic need of the individual is related to those things that tend to develop or redevelop and reconstruct individual capacity—education (I mean every ounce of it from which the individual is capable of profiting), vocational training, preventive medical care, habilitation and rehabilitation of the handicapped, physical restoration and appliances, vocational retraining, and readjustment. Another thing I would add to either grouping is the right of a handicapped individual to economic help in initiating some small independent business. These at least we need today and more in the future—minimum

99

standards of shelter, for example—as society's capacity continues to grow.

Mastery of the techniques that enable an individual to express himself at the optimum and the opportunity to employ his capacities is essential to preserve the personality and character of individuals. Our ancient Bill of Rights thus needs to be supplemented by legal guarantees that reflect the dependency of the individual upon his fellow men, in terms not alone of safeguards against positive injury but also for inclusion in those media which society has been called upon to supply for the support of its membership. The individual must regain the sense of living in an environment whose responses in areas essential to the support and development of his life are legally available and may not be capriciously withheld under the law.

It is to these ends that I would summon the ethical concepts and principles that I have sought to develop in the preceding pages. Because every individual is so deeply sensitive, and, no doubt, subconsciously concerned about the rock-bottom bases of his security—for which he is almost wholly dependent these days upon his fellow men—we seek to provide minimum guarantees in the form of firm commitments and to sustain them at feasible levels. These commitments, however, must always be envisaged as foundation points from which every individual remains free to rise and to seek whatever heights of attainment he may be able to achieve.

It is true that these commitments are a burden, a heavy burden, for they can be maintained only at a cost imposed in some appropriate ratio upon our economic capacity, a cost imposed not only in terms of money, but also in direct requisitions upon usable materials and skills. But we should become more vividly aware of the extent to which tradition has blinded us to the true economics of the welfare enterprise. It seems indeed unfortunate that because the whole process developed in ways divorced from the main stream of our socio-economic life, it has been conceived as something forcibly taken from the regular economy, independently supported by it, and imposed like a cost of government as an unalloyed burden upon it. This conception is, of course, ultimately quite false. We are even now becoming aware that the whole security process is properly an integrated part of our whole social and economic life. We are becoming aware, too, that there are very tangible economic advantages in the pooling of certain of our resources, a circumstance which is especially evident in the vastly more effective and efficient use that can thus be made of the ever costlier machines and instrumentalities which industry creates in this atomic age for the exploitation of nature and for the satisfaction of human needs. And it will be found that this saving becomes more and more noticeable as we proceed into the deeper and more poignant areas of human need, in refined medical and surgical operations, in biological research, in fields of specialized training, and in many other areas.

But, of course, we should not fool ourselves. Many attempts have been made to prove that there are immediate economic returns in social welfare operations that balance the cost. Such attempts have always come face to face with the obvious fact that the more poignant the need which social programs seek to meet, the more costly the operation becomes in relation to any direct or immediate economic return. In only one area has it been at all possible to demonstrate an immediate economic return, and that is in the rehabilitation process where it is sought to be shown that for a few hundred dollars, individual earning power in considerably greater amounts can be re-established. But in most areas there is a contrary principle involved. Take education, for example. Is it not obvious that the greatest economic return from the least expenditure is to be found in the training of the best potential skills and the brightest minds? The same principle holds in the broad health field and in other areas. The least return at the greatest expenditure will result from efforts to better standards at their lowest levels. Yet experience teaches us this is where the effort must be made if the true objectives of the welfare process are to be obtained and society fundamentally strengthened. We must get down to the lowest depths of our social foundations and work diligently at that point if we are to strengthen its structure; so the attempt to state the matter in terms of an immediate economic return is an indication of the short range of our vision.

It follows that the feasible levels of subsistence will be determined empirically and should be resolved as a problem secondary to the legal terms of the commitment. It would seem obvious, for example—and fully borne out, I believe, by experience—that higher standards of living are maintainable at a given cost in proportion as health needs are first met. To attempt the maintenance of relatively high subsistence standards while practicable health measures are neglected seems uneconomic. Thus society's concern with the provision of an effective and omnipresent medical service is amply attested. The fiscal question is not "Can we?" but "What can we?"

My concern as a lawyer from this standpoint, however, is rather to indicate some of the more essential legal principles which must be adhered to in the undertaking.

Chapter 8

ADMINISTRATION'S TASK—TO SERVICE LEGAL RIGHTS

LEGAL SCIENCE and the legal point of view affect in countless ways nearly all aspects of what we do to make society a
healthier environment for human beings, and for human personality and character development. But the point of first
consequence in my opinion is the conclusion that society
should actually commit or obligate itself to serve the life of
its individual members. This means that all social undertakings
as they constitute obligations of society constitute rights of
the individual. The individual then derives a sense of security
such as can come only from the knowledge that all human
life is committed to his own life.

I pointed out at the outset, however, that it is *society* and
not the *state* that is to undertake the commitment. There is
widespread confusion between the two. The phrase "Welfare
State," now in frequent use, was given currency by those who
would gladly compound this confusion. The reliance of the
individual is not upon the state but upon the society of which
he is a part.

Many individuals unthinkingly adopt the view that social
programming involves undertakings on the part of the *state*
as though the state was the primary obligor. Thus there is in

general a failure to accept social programs as a mere ordering of the acknowledged dependency, in modern times, of the individual upon his socio-economic environment. The tax power and public agencies of social administration are merely examples of the kind of tools which society may use to fulfill its own undertakings.

We must draw a sharp line, however, between the service of humanity and the maintenance of order. Public social administration brings a new picture of government into view. We must see it as an instrumentality for service rather than as an instrument of authority.

The idea that the state itself has become obligated in social undertakings leads to patent absurdities such as, for example, the belief that health services and economic security are a part of the "costs" of government. This again leads to the paradoxical view that by refusing to use the tax power to maintain private life, the legislature leaves more money outstanding to meet the needs of private life. Actually the tax power is used in such cases to assure that need will be met in the processes of distribution. The tax power is used as a control in the economic process. The point is to see that the needs of all are met. The rights of one individual are balanced against the rights of others.

EQUAL PROTECTION OF THE LAWS

The conception of a legal right and the idea of equality in legal treatment are complementary ideas. An excellent test of a right is the ability to demand equal treatment. We can usually tell whether or not our agency-client relationships are governed by law by finding out to what extent they are affected by the rules of equal protection. Our Constitution has no more significant function than to guarantee the "equal protection of the laws." If two individuals apply to you for something they need, neither one having any legal right to demand it, it is then your privilege to yield to one and to deny the other. But if both have a legal claim upon you, you can no longer choose capriciously to whom you will respond or what you will do. A demand as of right is always a demand for equal consideration.

The fact is that unless you have a clear right to something, you have no basis on which to challenge the justice or injustice of what is done or not done in your case. It is simply no business of yours. One should be grateful for a favor but may not be heard to complain that it is not granted. A Utah judge in an unreported case put the situation in a nutshell when he said, "The Attorney General contends that the law is constitutional and argues that old-age assistance is a charity to which no one is entitled as a matter of right. He contends that the legislature may give or withhold it as it sees fit and may divide recipients of old-age assistance into classes holding real property and those not holding real property, and require the one to promise to repay without so requiring the other class, and that by so doing there is no discrimination between the group. The sum and substance of the argument is that one 'should not look a gift horse in the teeth.'"

The equal protection of the laws, as the courts have often said, is grounded on the existence of a legal right. If there be no right, there can be no inequality in the legal sense, nor can anyone be conjured up who would have a standing in court to raise the question, for no one is legally hurt. All the cases that spell out the meaning of equal protection arise out of challenges and protests made by those who have legal rights and who can see the inequalities in what is done about them. The fact that the rule of equality applies as well to what is given by law as to what is taken away by law is obvious. The Constitutional mandate of equal protection requires that "All persons . . . shall be treated alike, under like circumstances and conditions, both in the privileges conferred, and in the liabilities imposed." [1] But actually a large portion of the few legal decisions that say so, have arisen in relation to one single issue. That issue is race discrimination in public education, for apparently there is a right as well as a duty to attend school. Only the fact that such a right has been conceived and expressed raises the issue of inequality in its satisfaction. But how many other affirmative claims upon society are there?

The significance of many of the most elemental facts about ourselves and our society is not appreciated. Take, for example, the fact that the equal protection of the laws is not observed in welfare activity generally, nor are the supporting statutes challenged for their failure to meet this basic test of constitutionality. I shall never forget the sense of incredulous amazement I experienced when I suddenly became aware of this fact. The fact itself is as paradoxical as the view which tolerates the payment of "charity" from the public treasury when the state constitution literally forbids it.

The reason, of course, is that most welfare activities were originally undertaken either as private undertakings, in which case they are not regarded as an integral phase of the socio-legal economy, or they have appeared as a phase of our efforts to safeguard the rights and the peace of the rest of society. Our conceptions of social justice will be revolutionized when we decide to make our social laws part and parcel of the legal framework of our society and apply the equal-protection-of-the-laws principle to the rights and opportunities thus created. At the moment, we just do not see the issue clearly enough to be disturbed by the injustice in what we do to promote justice. So we go on in happy satisfaction over each individual to whom we have done some good and expect those

1. *Truax* v. *Corrigan,* 257 U.S. 312, 333 (1921), quoting from *Hayes* v. *Missouri,* 120 U.S. 68 (1887). Cf. Smith, "Public Assistance as a Social Obligation," *Harvard Law Review,* vol. 63, no. 2, p. 275.

we pass over to take it in the true spirit of a sportsman at a roulette table.

One of the two or three situations or practices that I find most constantly irritating as a lawyer is the disposition of a legislature to appropriate a particular sum of money for the apparent purpose of "doing good" in some general field. Our legislators, for example, sit down year after year to decide how much, if any, money they will appropriate to implement a law passed a few years back to provide the necessary physical appliances, surgical treatment, and training to rehabilitate crippled children. The counties and states, conceived as units for the operation of this elemental duty of society, may have been authorized, as, indeed, they were in Title V of the Social Security Act, to receive funds in proportion to the number of crippled children who live in each of them, but no one knows how many there are and no one has undertaken up to this time to find out. The assumption is that whatever money and resources are made available for the purpose will find a need for their expenditure in any community; so why worry too much about how you apportion it? Besides that, the law says "crippled" children, and if you construe the term "crippled" broadly, there are of course plenty of crippled children. The law has not been drafted in terms precise enough to give definable rights to a definable group. So when the year goes by and it comes time to maintain the program for another season, the same question arises—shall anything be appropriated and if so how much?

Crippled children are one example of what has become a pattern. Other laws in the same vein concern themselves with the very subsistence of children, or of the aged or the ill, or the rehabilitation of the injured, or the guardianship of children, or the care of the sick. Society has an extensive job. Why think in terms of individuals!

Our high courts, however, say that the laws of the state "must be equal in their benefit as in their burden." [2] This means, the courts say, that "the distribution of the benefits must be made upon some fair and equal classification or basis." Unequivocal authority is cited for these propositions, but they are widely ignored and traditional conceptions carry on. These traditional conceptions sprang in part from the methods of private philanthropy, under which benefits were bestowed at will by the rich. They sprang also from the tenets of the police power, under which primitive social legislation was ascribed to the need to protect the established rights of the rest of society rather than to meet the needs of individuals for the individual's own sake. Neither law nor philanthropy was motivated by the aim of giving the individual a legal status and legal rights commensurate with his needs.

The failure to be precise in social measures, the hazy descriptions of those for whom some remedial good is intended, the lack of any serious attempt to match the available resources with the job that is cut out for them, are prime facts behind our current disregard of the principle of equal rights under law. This hesitancy to put the service of fundamental human needs on a legal footing still characterizes most of our social and political activity in the field of human welfare. The responsibilities loosely delegated by statute are almost never brought to a focus anywhere along the line. On the contrary, the customary failure of the legislative body to assume responsibility for defining the job, and paying for what it defines, opens the door to the uncontrollable impulses and demoralizing influences of sporadic prejudice and naive community attitudes about the deserving and the undeserving and what should or should not be done and to whom. These influences leave public agencies in a veritable vortex of conflicting views

2. See *Truax* v. *Corrigan*, 257 U.S. 312, 333 (1921).

and emotions, often with no obligation to defend those views before a legal tribunal.

So lacking in legal precision are the benefits of much social legislation that it is sometimes impossible to say whether some condition described in a statute is meant to bring somebody in or leave him out. I read a statute once which described a group of children as those living with neglectful and depraved parents. Actually it was impossible to say with certainty whether these children were intended to be included or excluded from the benefits of the law. I could not tell for sure whether the draftsman was bemoaning the child's plight or seeking to penalize the perverse social attitudes of the parent by the withholding of benefits from the child. Should the fact that a child's parents are aliens or refuse to undergo some training or surgical operation nullify the child's claim upon society? Again, if ten individuals meet the conditions of eligibility for rehabilitative treatment stated in a public statute, how does one go about selecting five? Do you keep your eyes half closed, toss a coin, or move to another community? Is a legislature free to require any length of residence within the state it pleases as a condition to the right of its inhabitants to the benefits of its welfare laws? Might a legislature provide medical services or economic security for only those individuals who were born in the state, for example? The only legal case I know of on this issue leaves the door wide open to such statutory curiosities.[3] Public schooling could not be so limited, for its constitutional status is recognized. Whenever you become a resident of a state, you would expect your children to be taught in its public schools. Schools, like other basic governmental services, are established for the benefit of all residents.

How does one justify the payment of cash assistance to one

3. *People ex rel. Heydenreich et al.* v. *Lyons,* 374 Ill. 557, 30 N.E. (2d) 46 (1940).

family and a mere order for the delivery of groceries to another? Is it sound to try to starve out a boarding home or an institution that does not maintain adequate standards, by refusing assistance to individuals who live there? Is it equal protection to try to make one person support another by denying assistance to the individual whose relative refuses to support him? Is it ethical to squeeze the individual who happens to lie under your thumb in order to bring pressure to bear on someone else? To paraphrase a well-known comment—It may be art, but is it clever, or is it pretty?

Such questions, of course, probe to the depths of our philosophy and motivation. Does society come first or the individual? We do not, I think, aid children as a social asset, in any ultimate sense. We must regard the individual as an end in himself. Our ethical justifications do not require reinforcement from social ends. May we not come to realize that society's greatest achievement is a mature, responsible, and highly competent individual?

To be sure, equal protection is something to guide us in what we do. In general it does not condemn us for what we do not undertake to do. But it does demand of us an answer to two questions. The first question to which it demands an answer is, Exactly what, specifically, have we undertaken to do? The second question is, Have we included or excluded individuals or groups for reasons that make sense in terms of what we have undertaken to do? These questions cannot be answered at all, or at all properly, in reference to the greater part of social legislation.

But in areas where law has undertaken, traditionally, and necessarily under the Constitution, to deal with people on an objectively equal basis it has achieved this goal through the age-old science of classification. I am speaking of classification for purposes of inclusion and exclusion and not for treatment purposes; but, for any purpose, it is the indispensable method of reaching just results.

To classify in the strict sense, you start by identifying certain criteria as the basis of your determinations. These criteria must bear a rational and logical relation to the primary objective of the law or program. Then as you proceed to apply these criteria in individual cases, you will identify, in terms of these criteria, a group whose treatment under the law or program will faithfully carry out the authorized objective. The crux of this method lies in comparing the criteria of exclusion or inclusion with the actual objectives of the law or program.

It is sometimes thought that the theory of classification restricts one's ability to limit the size of the group which any law affects. This is not true to the extent that the statutory objective can be narrowed. It is theoretically possible to confine the objective, and hence the group affected, ad infinitum. Many workers in the field of social science have urged the necessity for broadened administrative discretion or for the right to be capricious or selective on the ground that it is not possible to apply the constitutional guarantee of equal protection of the law in many new programs because the scope of inclusion must inevitably be much broader than financing or facilities will permit. Actually, however, the principle of classification gives the only true method of restricting the group. We must restrict our goals in accordance with criteria which will enable us invariably to explain the selection of one individual and the rejection of another within the strict rubric of our objective. The individual's right to be considered on an objectively sound basis must always be protected.

One of the most interesting tests of the process of classification of individuals that has come to my attention arose over the problem of the so-called "reservation Indians." Certain states with large reservation Indian populations, because of the relatively smaller tax contribution from such sources, were anxious to exclude reservation Indians from social laws. But of course Indians "as such"—i.e., as a race—could not be excluded, and other grounds of exclusion failed to accomplish the desired end when they were logically pursued. The exclusion of individuals living on reservations had the undesirable effect of excluding many white people living on reservations, a circumstance which confirmed the apparent illegality of such a residence differentiation. The attempt to exclude Indians as so-called "wards" of the Federal Government involved a difference in citizenship status and had the effect of excluding persons of Indian blood who were living throughout the state in normal private life. Differences in the nature of the needs of the Indian group or the fact of their reliance on the Federal Government fell before the plain facts of each individual case.

So in testing each criterion it became apparent that what you should do was to take two individuals, stand them up side by side, and determine with realism why you would choose one and reject the other. Thus a reservation Indian and a reservation white were placed side by side. It thus became apparent that you could not reject one and take the other on grounds rationally related to the statutory or program objective since both stood alike in their claim.

But the evil of which I speak is not a matter of race or creed or any other familiar ground of discrimination. It is deeper by far. It is a question of the right of society to be capricious as against the right of the individual to be objectively treated under law. No boast can be made that social programs are operating under and in accordance with the Constitution of the United States at the present time, or indeed until the time comes when it is possible for an individual who has been excluded or who is treated less favorably than another individual to present the matter to a court and to determine whether his treatment can be justified within the terms of the statutory objective when it is honestly compared with any other *single inclusion* that has been made under the statute. Then and then only will there be equal protection under the great body of statutory laws which control the expenditure of a goodly percentage of our tax funds.

The administrative task should be conceived in the main as a means of implementing the free and legitimate exercise of these rights in view of the number of individuals involved. The administrator should be the servant of the right, not its creator.

The individual should not be subject, as he generally is today, to the judgment of administrators and their employees as to the ethical basis of his individual right and the scope of his individual prerogative in any of these respects. In social parlance, today, the determination of his right to be included in any public social program is a part of what is called eligibility determination. The determination of an individual's eligibility is usually a complicated process. The decision often reflects the judgment of some administrative staff member. In the main, however, eligibility determination should be restricted to the kind of fact-finding process that a doctor engages in when he diagnoses physical conditions or the tax collector engages in when he determines economic conditions. What is needed, what law should supply, is a clear, unmistakable statement of the exercisable right of the individual written in advance upon the face of every pigeonhole into which the facts of his case may put him. And these legal rights and the obligation to fulfill them should always be referable to the judicial process so that if any conflict between law and human will or judgment arises, the issue will be objectively determined.

The course of development under which the courts were largely removed from the consideration of the most basic and elemental of human and individual rights, was due to the failure of the statute to answer the basic questions which it is the legislative responsibility to answer. It must first define what the individual is entitled to, and define it accurately enough so that a court can determine whether or not the right has been satisfied. It must assume responsibility for creating the right. It is for the legislature, and for the legislature alone, to determine whether there is an ethic or, as we may say, a moral obligation that should be converted into a legal obligation. Instead of defining rights, organized society delegated its responsibility, in the earlier and less urgent stages of the social problem, to superintendents of the poor (originally overseers). The very word "overseer" expresses the attitude that brought overseers into being. The discretion reposed in such local officials is of course utterly inconsistent with procedure under a positive code of human rights.

The human judgment and discretion that has traditionally entered into the consideration of the individual's claim deprives the individual of the ability to challenge administrative decisions. Unless society will commit itself, the courts obviously cannot touch the issue. Let there be no misunderstanding on this point. When I am given discretion to do one of several things—or nothing—whatever I decide to do satisfies the law. All the law called for was my decision and I made it. The decision is right because I made it, not because I was bound to decide that way. There is nothing by which a court can evaluate the rightness or wrongness of what I decided or what I did. There is no issue, in fact, for a court, unless you can present to the court a demonstrable statement of what you were entitled to and show to the court that an obligation exists to satisfy it.

The great reliance on what are called private charitable agencies in the meeting of the fundamental needs of human life attests the fact that society, itself, had not accepted the fact that the individual had a moral or ethical right to the satisfaction of these universal needs through social action.

114

Most of what has been done in the past has been done as "gifts above measure"—to use Browning's phrase in *Pippa Passes*—that is to say, above the measure of any moral or ethical entitlement or prerogative. Our ethics, and our charitable instincts, and our benevolent attitudes should be merged in our laws, and become integrated with them. We need to narrow the gap between the law and ethical action.

The lawyer and the social psychologist may well agree on the need to wipe completely from the minds of men this benevolence theory of social programming, this idea of a handout. It is, after all, nothing but a point of view, nothing at base but bad psychology or perhaps an attempt on these grounds to justify a very narrow conception of social obligation. The cure, therefore, is a fundamental reorientation of our thinking until we come to see that what individuals need they are entitled to, and that the chief end of social organization, as Jefferson said, is to see that they get it. What, after all, is the function of organized society if not to serve the needs of man and help him realize his aims?

An experience I can never forget was my talk with a representative of the American Bankers Association. Certain remarks of his in relation to a bill to institute federal grants for those seeking college and professional education had led me to believe that I might find here a real challenge to my point of view. I eagerly described to him the permanent loss I had suffered in my efforts to finance my own education in these respects—the frustration of a normal ambition to excel in certain areas where mental concentration was essential, the permanent impairment to eyesight from bad food and consequent strain, the temporary incursion of tuberculosis, and, more poignantly, the sacrifice of all that sense of power that breeds in the social group life of our higher institutions. To this I added my reaction to the false notions to which I was constantly subjected about the advantages of self-help endorsed by those who would contribute on a voluntary basis to "worthy" and "meritorious" seekers after knowledge. I wound up by expressing, without reservation, the conviction I had sustained ever since graduation, that every child born into our society was normally entitled, as his pure prerogative as a member of that society, to every ounce of free education that he could absorb.

To my amazement my whole personal story was more than matched by my banker friend's fight for knowledge and my resulting conviction was wholeheartedly and unreservedly shared by him. He had sought to emphasize the need to answer, in the present state of legislative thinking, the fiscal facts that were being used to support the contentions of those who would send their children forth under such financial burdens and handicaps to institute their careers and their families.

Reporters and editorial writers sometimes use the phrase "voluntary benevolence" to describe the activities of private social agencies. One is led to inquire at once whether there is such a thing as "involuntary benevolence"! Public welfare has, perhaps, been so conceived. But we still act voluntarily when we take the legal road. What we do, essentially, is to commit ourselves to the ethic we profess.

From the converse standpoint, the distinction we need always to emphasize is the one between law and uncoordinated social action. The weaknesses of uncoordinated social action are most apparent when you consider the need for some standard to guide the individual who is asked to contribute to social action. What is the measure of his obligation?

Individuals generally wish to make some contribution to a worthy cause, but when, as is normally the case, it involves sacrifice, they need to know what the just division of the burden requires of them. They know that in the long run they cannot find their satisfaction in popular approval of what they do, or in a competition of giving. But there is a strong sense of duty in all individuals. This sense of duty demands to know what that duty is.

We need the right to act in the knowledge of what is expected of us and what we may expect of others. We need to regard law as a standard-setting agency rather than as an unseating or dethronement of our own freedom of action. We need to express our valid social impulses in our laws. We need to stop asking individuals to beg for the right to live while condemning them for being beggars.

I am aware that the more successful we are in reducing human needs to human rights, the less administration we will need in the sense in which laymen think of the administrative process. We should recognize that the processes of administration are merely tools for effectuating rights that exist independently of the means of satisfying them. The administrator's primary job is to determine the facts in the individual case. His second major responsibility is to devise means for satisfying, on an individual basis, yet equitably as between individuals, rights that under modern social laws apply to large categories of individuals. Our fact-finding processes and our distributive processes are vital factors in promoting social welfare. Fact-finding implies a great deal of equipment today, and, as there are a great many of us, the satisfaction of our needs of whatever nature implies organization on a scale commensurate with the undertaking. For these purposes we need the administrative process. A degree of objectivity in the administrative process in dealing with the needs and resources of individuals is essential. The conditions under which claims are processed and individual treatment is accorded, must be such as to form the basis for an appeal to the courts by any individual who believes that he has not received what he is entitled to procure.

Our law expresses our philosophy, as judicial cases mirror our human lives. Until a philosophy of life motivates justice as it is expressed by our judges, it cannot be counted as a ruling principle in our society. That this is true is our salvation. Let us then strive to encompass social measures in the scope of our fundamental legal guaranties of equal protection and the right to be heard under law.

SELF-DETERMINATION

From the policy standpoint our main concern should be to promote the individual's assumption of responsibility for the issues of his life. I am aware that the symbolization of all material things in terms of money is one of the most potent of all factors in preserving an individual's freedom in the management of his own affairs. An individual who has the necessary cash is not limited to one source of supply when others exist. He thus obtains a freedom of choice that the attempt to satisfy his needs directly by supplying him with the material thing itself does not allow him.

We have in our social programs today what we call cash programs and what we call service programs. The Social Security Act, in its espousal of economic security, brought a large measure of freedom, first in expressing security benefits in terms of legal rights of the individual, and secondly in defining those legal rights in terms of cash—purchasing power rather than things purchased, and so giving to the individual both the right and the responsibility of choice in meeting his needs.

The goal of independence teaches that the question of whether or not an individual's security is best promoted through the assurance of cash income, is to be answered in terms of the freedom of choice you can thus preserve to the individual. Unquestionably when you are talking about the ordinary needs of life, the element of individual choice is vital. You cannot supply in kind the ordinary requirements of living without exercising over those who receive them, as over those who produce them, many of the responsibilities of guardianship. This is because you are reaching down to the things that motivate the most detailed and intimate acts and decisions of existence.

There is a great deal of confusion about the relation of need, in the sense of lack of financial resources, to the establishment of a public service program such as medical and surgical care or treatment. If by need you mean lack of money, there is, in pure logic, one and only one answer to that—the supplying of money—cash. If by need you mean the need of a surgeon's skill, you will, in pure logic, satisfy that need only by supplying the services of the skilled surgeon. Having done so, the need is satisfied and the want of money or the possession of money has not entered into the picture. Yet it is often, perhaps generally, considered that all human needs are definable in economic terms. Medical need, for example, is defined in economic terms with the admonition that a medically needy individual is not necessarily as poor as the individual who needs money for food, clothes, fuel, and other things. He just has not funds enough to purchase the medical care he needs.

The law, however, has for centuries found it necessary to distinguish between rights that money will presumably satisfy and those that it will not satisfy. If you have contracted for the services of an opera singer, money damages will not make you whole, and the law, in agreement with this obvious fact, will endeavor to get you the unique thing you bargained for. The converse of this is seen in the fact that you cannot, in an industrialized economy, supply in terms other than money the same opportunities that a cash income supplies. To do so, practically everything would have to be free for the asking. We express our individuality in the common pursuits and accoutrements of life. There is therefore a sound basis for the distinction between cash and service programs.

Medical care should be a service program because in many respects medical service is unique. It is not invariably duplicable for a given amount of money. The only alternative is to make it an insurance program with everybody insured so that the variable incidence and cost are spread throughout society and adjusted, in their impact, to capacity. But then you still have the distributional problem with respect to the services, as well as the problem of providing safeguards in relation to quality, as to which most laymen want guidance. It happens here that the table d'hôte is less restrictive than the à la carte method. Public service is freer than a private operation under numerous discrete controls.

But the point that concerns me most is the establishment of the individual's right to the service. How can such a right be effectuated as a right? From the security standpoint, this is as important as, perhaps in this field more important than, it is in relation to the daily wants of life. The aim of security is not advanced by subjecting the individual to an argument as to whether he is worthy of the service, whether the condition from which he suffers was brought on by his own negligence, or whether he is going to want a second operation when he succeeds in getting the first one. Only if he is getting the treatment as a matter of right and not as so-called charity will he escape the thrust of such a debate. Individuals with rights do not get themselves involved in discussions of this kind. One cannot object, of course, to the authoritative establishment of the facts on which a right is founded, but the factual diagnosis, when made in the wake of established law, should end all discussion as to the individual's right.

In general, the right to medical care can be made effective only by setting up a service program, in which rights to medical treatment are defined and services to satisfy them are made available. You can do this if you can acquire the requisite medical skills and preserve in the process such prerogatives of choice as an individual needing a specialized service can possibly wield. If you insist that the right be set up only for those without money, you have some way and somehow drawn a distinction between individuals in terms of money in areas where money has no relevancy. The premise that one individual can pay for the service from other resources and another cannot is utterly void of significance as the test of a right established to meet a need that is not economic in its nature. It overlooks the fact that the creation of a legal right to the service puts both individuals in exactly the same situation.

Chapter 9

GUARDIANSHIP AND STATUS OF CHILDREN

T HE LAW, in building its structure of right and obligation around the individual, proceeds, as we have seen, upon the basic assumption that all individuals are responsible for the fulfillment and satisfaction of their personal rights and obligations. Since this is certainly not true in fact of infants and incompetents, the law has had of necessity to devise some means of maintaining its major premise in these situations. It, therefore, adopted the institution of private guardianship. This has been its historic method of avoiding state guardianship. Private guardians are appointed by the judiciary and are responsible to the judiciary. Executive controls are thus eliminated and the rule of law safeguarded.

This structure and institution is, at the present time, gravely threatened. The threat arises from the very fact that society, suddenly conscious of its duty toward the individual, has instituted many varied activities called social programs in which it seeks to meet certain of his primary needs. The common view is that these programs are functions of the state. The professional role played by the state as a mere tool of society is not popularly regarded as significant. Some administrators have proceeded on the general premise that the paramount objective is to meet need, whatever the effect upon individual pre-rogative. Furthermore, the conditions under which these social programs have been instituted, the failure, or at least the delay, in integrating them with the traditionally recognized rights of the individual, has exaggerated the administrative role. Certain agencies, like the Bureau of Public Assistance in the Social Security Administration, have met with much prejudice in their efforts to encourage a more objective viewpoint. Account must be taken of the fact that most of the beneficiaries of these so-called programs are to be found in the lower ranks of competence. These programs were intended to strike at the base of society. Their aim is to raise minimum standards. The result, in view of the decadence of private guardianship procedure and the general lack of understanding of its function, is that the state has moved wholeheartedly into the areas of private planning and the management of private economies in such manner as to constitute a grave threat to democratic principles. This is the vital problem that confronts us when we seek to envisage the future of such programs as social security, child welfare, and all phases of individual rehabilitation.

Indeed, the modern security system and the discovery, development, and proffer of services, whether medical, educational, or economic, which are opening up new vistas of life and hope to the weaker elements of our society, place an entirely new emphasis upon the ability of those entitled to these new rights to take the kind of action and make the elections and decisions that these opportunities require. We are creating rights that did not previously exist and we are bestowing them upon individuals who did not previously possess such prerogatives and who in many instances need more than professional guidance in exercising them. The assumption of responsibility for the determination of individuals who have themselves lost all power to view their own situation objectively, should be undertaken only by those who are accountable judicially for their actions—for they are become their brother's keeper.

Our concern with legal incapacity stretches all the way from the need for consents to some treatment or dealing with the individual or his economy, through the need for reliable commitments and assumptions of obligation, the need for decisions and action essential to the individual's exercise of rights, the demand for releases of liability for risks that others may not wish to assume with respect to the child, and finally to the basic concerns of individual security, personal supervision, and status. The general assumption that underlies all human law is that the individual, possessed of legal rights and obligations, is able to express himself in legal terms and to maintain his individual identity and status in society. Ideally, every individual should constitute at all times an effective legal personality, so that relationships are governed by law.

A guardian is sometimes called a substitute parent or a legal parent. The individual chosen to act as guardian is given letters of authorization from a court, as is an executor, for example. Pursuant to this authority he is enabled to act with or to represent his ward whose legal personality he thus supplements or protects. It is entirely feasible to provide a flexible system to meet the particular needs of the individual. Guardianship lacks the rigidity and permanency of an adoption and may be fulfilled without legally assuming the duty of financial support, for which other resources, such as the Social Security system envisages, may be made available.

However, it is quite true that society, especially our own Anglo-Saxon system, has egregiously failed to maintain the individual legal status and human rights of children; and, of course, married women were greatly limited in the exercise of legal prerogatives, especially in relation to their property concerns. So neglectful has society been in protecting children that their legal status has very properly been compared to that of a chattel, the legal right to which is generally coincident with its possession. Incredibly this is still true of children whose natural parents are dead or have abandoned them. It is a great fallacy to suppose that this situation can be corrected by administrative action. The law itself is at fault. Appreciation of the law's failure to protect children may be gained from consideration of the misleading concept known as *in loco parentis.*

Seeing or hearing this phrase, *in loco parentis*, one would think it described some kind of formal relationship. Actually it implies no more than legal recognition of a temporary situation that in point of fact happens to exist. It implies only that the child has come into the possession of someone who has undertaken for the time being to care for him. It postulates the existence of parental rights only while the care continues.

As Chief Justice Rugg, construing a statute in Massachusetts, said in *Coakley* v. *Coakley*: "... there is no continuing obligation on one who has assumed such a relation. It may be abandoned at any time." [1]

The result is that while the law is so solicitous of natural parenthood as to make it doubtful in many jurisdictions that a complete abandonment and termination of the rights of a natural parent can ever be effectuated, yet once this is achieved through death or otherwise, the child is thereafter transferrable on delivery over of his body. Having no adopted parent or legal guardian, his only relationship is an "in loco parentis" relationship which carries with it almost no legal security, none whatsoever beyond the passing hour. Thus, being once abandoned, the child may have no actual haven except in the hands of some public or private agency that cares

1. 216 Mass. 71, 102 N.E. 930, at 932 (1913). For other cases showing the impermanence of this relationship see *Wood* v. *Wood*, 166 Ga. 519, 143 S.E. 770 (1928); *Schaedel* v. *Reibolt*, 33 N.J. Eq. 534.

for stranded waifs. Presumably the child cannot be affirmatively thrown out upon the street, but as the law stands he has no security. It is above all else the promise of a future that a growing child demands.

It has been said, for example, that there is "no such thing as a *parent* (this means a natural parent) 'giving' custody of his own child to another, in the sense that under no circumstances could he again have custody of the child solely because of this alleged gift." This is a summation of common law doctrine. But modern statutes, largely motivated by the purpose to foster and protect the practice of placement and supervision of children by modern social and family welfare agencies, and in order to facilitate adoption (a comparatively recent addition to family law in English speaking countries), sometimes provide a legal basis for the termination of parental rights.

As Professor Sayre properly emphasizes, the parent-child relationship is not a property right that can be "sold or possessed like a haunch of beef." [2] Of course, it ought not to be. Any relationship with essentially personal involvements—a parent-child relationship above all others—carries with it collateral incidents of vital importance. To protect them, personal relationships must of necessity be legally formalized. It is these incidents of relationship, not the physical body of a child, that really constitutes the human *res*. They should be our real concern from the scientifically legal standpoint.

Then what, beyond its disregard of the basic demands of human security, does the present law signify? The answer is that common law provides no adequate means of protecting the human *res*. The fact that there may remain a vestigium of right in the former natural parent which provides the basis for an option of recovery—whether that option is derived from the old common law or the "best interests of the child" doc-

2. Paul Sayre, "Awarding Custody of Children," *University of Chicago Law Review*, IX (1941), 672, 676.

trine—does not relieve the stark fact that the child, *without an actively interested* parent, can in fact be delivered from person to person "like a haunch of beef." What is more, the possession of the recipient would not appear to be subject to question except where the facts of a particular case may demand the exercise of the police power.

That, indeed, is why social workers have been trying in vain, by administrative means, or through aid of the criminal law, to end the traffic in babies. But it is the civil law, not the criminal law, that is at fault, for it protects an individual who acquires merely the physical possession of the child.

The undesirable consequences of this traffic in children arise from the fact that they may be placed in unsatisfactory homes, and also from the fact that the prospective parents may find themselves with mentally or physically defective children. Legislation to correct this situation has generally taken the form of statutes forbidding the placing out of children for adoption without a license by the state. Some of these statutes prohibit all persons, including the natural parents, from placing out children, while others permit placing by natural parents and certain close relatives. In addition, some of these statutes prohibit the paying or receiving of compensation in connection with the placing of a child. The difficulties in effecting the cure through such legislation are obvious. The statutes which prohibit all unlicensed placing thereby attempt to vest complete power over the placement of children for adoption in licensed agencies. This exclusive grant of authority to such groups, whether they be private agencies or public administrative bodies, seems highly questionable, for such a power with its profound influence over human relationships, should, it would seem, be better left in the courts. Moreover, such a system would deprive natural parents of the right to select adoptive homes for their children. For example, suppose a mother should decide that a particular family whom she knows should adopt

her child. It seems questionable to authorize a third party, such
as one of these licensed agencies, to forbid such a placement.
Unless it be shown that the family which the mother had
selected is unfit to rear the child, should not the mother's
wishes be respected? It may be that the licensed agency would
in practice generally approve the placement unless the proposal was obviously bad. But that is no answer. The existence
of so arbitrary a power is enough to condemn it. Some legislatures have recognized the impropriety of depriving the
mother of her right to place out her child and have forbidden
only the placing-out activities of unlicensed third parties. The
question arises whether such a statute is violated by activities
undertaken to aid the mother in doing what it is legally per-
missible for her to do.

Some statutes prohibit anyone's paying or receiving compensation in connection with the placement. But valuable
service is worthy of being compensated, and there is nothing
essentially wrong in the mother's receipt of money upon giving up her child. She suffers economic loss. May not a prospective parent by operation of law properly pay medical
expenses connected with the birth, in which case ought not
liberal amounts be permitted in the interest of the child's care?
Opinions may differ sharply on this point, but it would seem
that the general condemnation of the paying or receiving of
compensation for child placement might well have the effect
of discouraging the rendering of adequate medical services.
If the mother is allowed to receive compensation, it seems
anomalous to prohibit the third party, who brought the
mother and the prospective parents together, from being compensated. It is not the money involved that constitutes the evil
to be cured; it is the unsatisfactory placements.

Convictions even under laws as well drafted as the New
York law, are proverbially difficult to obtain; and even where
the receiving of compensation has been outlawed, the fact that

in many cases the defendants must be conceded to have performed legitimate services, either as lawyers or as doctors, increases the difficulty. However, in a notorious case, which arose out of the much publicized airplane baby traffic between Florida and New York, certain defendants, including the lawyer involved, were convicted in New York of violating several of the provisions of the New York Penal Law and the Social Welfare Law. Defendant Slater's principal defense, that he was being paid only for his professional services as a lawyer for the mother and the prospective adoptive parents, was left for the jury to evaluate as a pure question of fact; the trial court charged that the statute was as applicable to lawyers as it was to others. The conviction was no doubt greatly aided by the fact that the mothers had been paid nominal amounts (which, however, may not have been measured by the amount of the lying-in expenses), whereas the recipients of the children paid from $1500 to $2000 in each case. "You bought low and sold high," said the prosecutor repeatedly, seeking to counteract the claim that the money was paid as a professional fee.

It is an interesting fact, as appears from the record of the Slater case, that in no case were the recipients of the children thus procured through Slater's connivance denied the privilege of adopting the child when they thereafter applied to the probate court. It is quite likely that such of the recipients as chose to adopt their babies, waited some time before filing their petitions for adoption, thus creating a situation which constrained the court, looking to the best interests of the child, to grant the petition for adoption. Other indictments have followed.

It should be noted that the difficulties involved in obtaining a conviction in the Slater case, the skillful techniques that were required of the prosecutor, plus the fact that the children remained in the homes Slater acquired for them for many months prior to the petitions for adoption, only serve to indicate the impracticality of the present statutory measures.

It is clear, therefore, that licensing statutes coupled with penal sanctions are not the answer. The solution to the problem is to be found by requiring that judicial authorization, based upon a finding that it would be in the child's best interests, precede any acceptance of the personal custody and control of a child. In other words, it should be illegal for anyone to hold in his possession, under a claim of personal right, the body of a child of which he was neither natural guardian nor adoptive parent without having been granted temporary or permanent letters of guardianship. At least one of our state legislatures has recently, in succinct terms, done exactly this. On March 19, 1951, a bill became law in the State of Washington which contains the following provision:

> It shall be unlawful for any person, partnership, society, association, or corporation, except the parents, to assume the permanent care, custody, or control of any minor child unless authorized so to do by a written order of a superior court of the state. It shall be unlawful, without the written order of the superior court having first been obtained, for any parent or parents to in any wise relinquish or transfer to another person, partnership, society, association, or corporation the permanent care, custody, or control of any minor child for adoption or any other purpose, and any such relinquishment or transfer shall be void: PROVIDED, That waivers and relinquishments heretofore signed by the parent or parents of said children or child shall be given the same force and effect as would be given prior to the enactment of this law.[3]

Of course it would be necessary for the court, before granting custody, to have the testimony of experts in the field of child welfare who have thoroughly investigated both the prospec-

3. State of Washington, *Laws of 1951*, chap. 251.

tive foster parents and the child, so as to insure that the interests of all concerned would be safeguarded and furthered by the granting of custody. If this concept were adopted with its resulting abridgment of the *in loco parentis* doctrine, we would be able to solve the problems of the traffic in babies with which so many of us are concerned.

Of course such a statute has significance far beyond the baby traffic problem. It is a most significant social reform. It portends the end of *in loco parentis* and the legal assurance of status for every child.

In the absence of "owners," for example, children have in the past "escheated" to the state very much as property escheated to the state in the absence of authorized personal recipients. This would seem to be the general theory under which children have been "committed" for centuries to public agencies and institutions authorized to hold them upon delivery. In fact, until relatively recent years, even a custodial institution itself, to whom children were committed, was not concerned to obtain a defined legal status in relation to the child such as guardianship implies. They undertook merely to carry certain publicly assumed responsibilities for caring for and finding homes for children under a statute. The child, being constituted a responsibility of the executive branch of government, becomes in very truth a ward of the state. The significance of this situation is that there is no automatic protection of the individual child. He has the same reliance as a domestic animal in respect of his ability to appeal to the protective safeguards of law. He can be and has been even more successfully exploited. *He has no guardian.*

Actually there may, therefore, have been some evidence of social progress in the fact that a number of states, and the District of Columbia, adopted at the turn of the century a type of statute the general purpose of which was to establish Boards of Public Guardians. Such boards were usually given general guardianship of all children "committed" by a court. In a typical New Jersey statute, for example, where the board was called the State Board of Children's Guardians, the agency was given "general supervision over all children adjudged public charges who may now or hereafter be in charge, custody, and control of any county asylum, county home, alms house, poor house, charitable hospital, relief or training institution, home or family to which such child or children may be or have been committed, confined, apprenticed, indentured or bound out." [4] This type of legislation has not been greatly modified. The child who is placed with a foster mother after being committed by the judge to a Welfare Department or Board of Children's Guardians, lies at the base of a kind of hierarchy of supervisory authorities.

The much-discussed juvenile courts of the country stand midway between the legal tradition and the private social tradition. They often represent an attempt to combine elements of the judicial and the administrative function. Individually, they veer from one conception of their role to another, depending more on the preferences of the judge than upon any statutory differences. Some regard themselves as the committed child's personal guardian; some maintain close relationships with the training schools, while others work more through the agencies. Few, if any, deem it of first importance to see that the child before them without parental guardianship has a suitable guardian or any guardian or utilizes guardianship as a method of procedure.

The Standard Juvenile Court Act, sponsored by the National Probation and Parole Association, provides a basis for carrying on this tradition although under its terms the court would also be given the authority to issue letters of guardianship. Section 18, clause 2, reads in part as follows:

4. State of New Jersey, *Laws of 1936*, C. 33, § 1, p. 74. The board was originally established by New Jersey in 1899 (*Laws of 1899*, p. 362).

... the court may * * * Commit the child to the custody or to the guardianship of a public or private institution or agency authorized to care for children or to place them in family homes, or under the guardianship of a suitable person. Such commitment shall be for an indeterminate period but in no event shall continue beyond the child's twenty-first birthday. . . .

In 1949 the U.S. Children's Bureau made a report of its study of guardianship in six states.[5] In these states some 250,000 children were found living in non-relative homes. The number of these provided with legal guardianship was so small as to be without significance. Also the Children's Bureau has obtained, on a voluntary basis, reports from many juvenile, county, and other courts dealing with children throughout the country. When projected over the country, those reports currently indicate that about 545,000 children are dealt with by these courts annually, and of them about 90,000 children are being committed or referred annually by our courts either directly to training schools and institutions or to public and private agencies for disposition. No doubt the majority of the latter are being "placed" in foster homes. Some of these homes are known as "free" homes and some as "boarding" homes. Of the total number of these children four out of every five are behavior cases while the other twenty per cent join the ranks of so-called "dependent" children for other reasons, including in some cases mere lack of support.

Recourse to guardianship procedure would have the effect of establishing the greater part of these foster relationships under the auspices of the juvenile or other guardianship court. It would involve much closer relationships between the social and welfare agencies and the court in establishing the relation-

5. *Guardianship, A Way of Fulfilling Public Responsibility for Children,* Children's Bureau Publication, No. 330 (1949).

ship. It would involve a much greater concern on the part of the court and its advisers for its success and future usefulness. But the individual child would become a ward of his foster parents and would cease to be regarded as a "ward of the court"; for that is the way courts work. They seek to establish self-operative instrumentalities and relationships. The parties, however, are always at liberty to go back to the court for important decisions and for protection and must do so for purposes of review, accounting, and evaluation.

The foster parent would become directly responsible to the court, but his relationship with his ward would be capable of standing on its own legs. The techniques of the modern social agency would not be less but more effectively used in the manner of all professional services. But the symbol of authority, and of deciding power, and ultimate responsibility for the future of the child would be cast upon the court and its judicially responsive instrumentalities. Under our system of constitutional government the judicial system, as one of its key functions or purposes, places the exercise of authority under appropriate safeguards. The judicial is the appropriate creator and sponsor of authoritative human relationships. I do not mean that individual social workers should not act as guardians any more than that lawyers should refrain from acting as trustees. But the professional function and the authoritative function should be separately organized, and this requires that all authoritative relationships be formalized and made judicially accountable.

I am not suggesting that child wards should be less frequently visited, nor am I suggesting that one jot or tittle be subtracted from the social and scientific skills and techniques that are brought to bear for the benefit of the ward and for the success of the relationship. I am merely saying that this ministry should be kept on a simon-pure professional basis; and to insure that this is the case, it is essential that the actual

134

guardian should be aware of his or her legal responsibility for the ward, and should be and remain accountable to the court, not to a social agency, and *a fortiori* not to a social worker.

A human being is, we know, deeply, profoundly, sensitive. One can be sure that children are fundamentally affected by any abnormality or insecurity in their family relationships though they probably could not begin to explain it or consciously realize it. Their relationships largely determine their personality attitudes. On this fact child psychology founds many of its conclusions. Law and the judicial power seem here to be failing in one of their most important functions, for it is through their instrumentality that these wounds must be ultimately treated.

Chapter 10

The Need for Private Personal Guardianship

No relationship is of greater significance to the social scientist who reveres the ideal of individual and private responsibility in a democracy, than private personal guardianship. Today no social reform seems more urgently needed than its re-creation, development, and greatly extended use. The reason is this:

Private life must not be managed or supervised by public bodies. Public agencies and professional organizations must not be allowed to dictate the views and decisions of individuals in matters of personal concern. Normal individuals possess the necessary competence to run their own lives, but children and incompetent adults do not. In fact, individuals exhibit varying degrees of competence. Alleged profligacy in the fields of his domestic economy has become one of the primary excuses used by society to justify its failure to come to the support of the individual. Lack of good management in domestic affairs is proverbial. Hence, there is a quite understandable tendency, once one has undertaken the business of running other peoples' lives, to become rather inclusive in defining the range of one's assumed responsibilities. One begins by becoming a kind of *de facto* guardian to some incompetent individual or child, and then graciously extends the "service" to individuals at every level of competence. Nearly all of us become at one time or another eligible for this kind of help. Indeed the traditional concern to see that individuals make the best use of other peoples' charity furnishes a point of departure in the more modern development of case work psychology.

The views and considerations affecting adult incompetency are of the same order or urgency as are those affecting children. There is ground for the belief that the individual's guardianship problem should, as a matter of law, have to be the first order of business in any case where the behavior of any individual child or incompetent adult is brought in question.

Attitudes towards adult guardianship are born very largely of the repulsive feeling about so-called "insanity" and the superstitious dread in which it has been regarded. Thus the stigma attached to the finding of incompetency upon which the service of guardianship has been conditioned, and indeed the nature of the proceeding itself, have all combined to blind us to the role which this legal institution is designed to play. The emphasis has been upon the legal establishment and declaration of incompetency and not upon maintaining legal capacity and providing the individual with the means of expression and protection.

It should be borne in mind that there are at the moment of writing some eight million individuals in our society who are mentally ill. While modern research is providing us with considerable knowledge with respect to mental health and illness, there is apparently no survey which would indicate the percentage of this group needing guardianship. Obviously the number would depend among other things on one's definition of incompetency and one's conception of the service of guardianship. It is well established factually that many persons are competent in one respect but quite incompetent in another. They might be held to be "competent to manage their affairs," I assume, yet, because of the nature of a mental illness, find themselves quite incapable of an objective decision with respect to their need for medical treatment and of any true expression of individual will with respect to it. In any event, the number of adults in need of the kind of service and safeguards that personal guardianship was intended to provide would number in the millions.

The hospitalization of the mentally ill has always posed serious problems, however inadequately met. Its legal implications are among its most serious aspects. An important step taken to promote satisfactory solutions of certain legal problems, for example, has resulted in the recent release of a draft act "Governing Hospitalization of the Mentally Ill," prepared in the Federal Security Agency (now the Department of Health, Education, and Welfare) by the National Institute of Mental Health, Public Health Service, and the Office of the General Counsel. The foreword, describing the scope of the Draft Act, contains the following with respect to guardianship:

> ... Decision as to hospitalization in the individual case, however, is one which as a rule needs to be made in the light of the individual's entire situation, including the availability of alternatives which may be sufficient or preferable, even from the medical point of view, in the particular case. In those cases where a guardian of the person has previously been appointed, the guardian should be helpful and will have a more or less authoritative role, depending upon the law of the State of the sick individual. Appointment of a guardian by the court may frequently be a desirable first step in meeting problems growing out of the individual's mental condition of which his need for hospitalization may be only one.

The Act, however, does not deal with guardianship as such,

The Need for Guardianship

nor does it make the status of incompetency a prerequisite to, or a consequence of, hospitalization....

Moreover, I think that if the previous appointment of a guardian were a condition precedent to all proceedings for involuntary hospitalization whether or not the proceeding was necessary to protect society—indeed if special guardians could be appointed with defined responsibilities in particular kinds of mental illness without the rigid and conclusive effects attributable under existing law to finding of legal incompetency, it might well be that many compulsive proceedings would prove unnecessary. In this connection it should be noted that Section 6 of the Draft Act contains a provision under which any individual may be admitted to a mental hospital upon written application, which application may be made by his guardian upon the certification of two designated qualified examiners that he is in need of such care.

The crucial section of the Draft Act, however, is Section 9. This section provides in part that "if, upon completion of the hearing and consideration of the record, *the court finds that the proposed patient*... is in need of custody, care or treatment in a mental hospital, and, because of his illness, lacks sufficient insight or capacity to make responsible decisions with respect to this hospitalization, it shall order his hospitalization for an indeterminate period, or for a temporary observation period...." (Italics mine.)

The fact that the issue as to hospitalization is thus resolved by providing for its determination *by the court in each individual case*, appears to convert the guardianship issue at this point into the mere question whether or not a guardian *ad litem* should be appointed. In any event, believing as I do that the institution of private guardianship provides an essential service to the individual, and that the appointment of a guardian should precede any authoritative dealing with the individual, especially institutionalization and treatment for an indefinite period, my own view would be that any such compulsive proceeding should be conditioned on the fact that the individual was assured of an opportunity to be present at a hearing, or if incapable of effective expression, to be present in the person of his guardian. Apparently an enlightened court, unless deeming itself to be for some reason without authority to do so, would see to it almost as a matter of course that the individual would have the protection of a guardian *ad litem* in a proceeding to determine hospitalization of an individual for a serious mental condition.

Accepting, for example, the view that a decision such as the hospitalization and treatment of an individual should be made only in the context of the entire pattern of his life and that the purpose of any such decision should be to reflect, as far as it is possible to ascertain it, the personal will of the individual, or at least to make determinations in the light of all that can be ascertained about his preferences, as well as his need for a type of treatment, and having regard to the fact that professional treatment implies a patient capable of assuming responsibility for decisions, it seems to me that personal guardianship is a vital need of the individual in this situation.

While it is true that any individual can hire expert advice as long as he is capable of an objective view of his own condition and problem, this is, nevertheless, just what a mentally ill person cannot do. Wisely imparted pressure by one who is judicially accountable is an important service. In dealing with this extensive borderline group, doctors almost of necessity become authoritative and overstep the bounds of purely professional behavior. The maintenance of professional attitudes, not only among doctors, but among all professions in social fields, requires, at the client end of the professional relationship, the presence of an integral personality, one capable of assuming responsibility for decisions. For this reason I think that courts have a responsibility, particularly important at the present juncture of our social history, for seeing that individuals are provided with the services of a personal guardian to represent them in an issue in which their mental condition is in question or where they are believed by competent medical authority to be incapable of a responsible decision. Such a protection might, I think, be provided without depriving the individual of the personal exercise of all his civil rights—but I wish first to stress the fact that our modern social legislation has brought this whole issue into focus.

When the Social Security Act was passed, there were, for example, over seven hundred individuals in Illinois eligible by reason of their age for old-age security payments, who under a curious but not unfamiliar statutory provision were compelled to suffer their maintenance income to be paid, not to them, but for their account to so-called "responsible persons." These "responsible persons" were a curious kind of administratively appointed guardian without any letters of guardianship, or written undertaking. The Social Security Administration, following the spirit as well as the letter of the Social Security Act, naturally refused Federal participation in such cases, a fact which influenced the state to abandon the practice in federally-aided programs. As a result the great majority of those for whom responsible persons had been appointed began to receive the payments in their own right. A few exhibited a need for judicial guardianship.

The attitudes that prompted this "responsible persons" involvement are strong enough, apparently, to prostitute even a normal guardianship procedure. In the State of Minnesota a guardianship statute[1] permitted an individual to apply to the court for a guardian of himself.[2] He would need, in the language of the statute, to allege that he himself was

1. *Minn. Rev. Stat.* §§ 525.54, 525.541.
2. *Scott* v *Whitely*, 168 Minn. 74, 209 N.W. 640 (1926).

"incompetent" or at least "wasteful and debauched." The welfare agency in that state found this statute useful because it seemed to enable them to say to the individual that upon his application to the court and upon the appointment of a guardian thereunder he might qualify for assistance, otherwise not. His legal right, if it could be so described, was actually conditioned upon his securing a guardian under the statute. The proceeding under the statute was supposed to be "voluntary." Is it then surprising that a small financial institution was used as guardian and became a sort of law arm of the Department of Public Welfare? Through its personnel the agency was able to control the expenditure of the benefits to which the individual was entitled under the statute. It seems to me that whether or not this practice pleases or sickens one will depend upon the nature of his social conscience.

Now obviously the bank in the above situation was either acting actually as a personal, not a property, guardian or else it was acting merely as an arm of the Department which, without appointment as such, was acting in fact as a personal guardian.

Thus there are two primary motivations. One is the practical need for legal capacity to make decisions and assume responsibilities; the other stems from the profounder implications of social policy.

Our legal system is founded upon the conception of a legal personality. Each individual becomes a node in the socio-legal pattern, a center from which obligations emanate and to which legal rights pertain. The great importance of this to the development of individualism is reflected in the assurance contained in Article 6 of the Universal Declaration of Human Rights. The language in which this article is phrased appeared in the earliest drafts of the declaration and again in the final draft in substantially unmodified form. It reads: "Everyone has the right to recognition everywhere as a person before the law."

But these conclusions are also grounded in the practical implications of guardianship as a social method and its deeper implications from the standpoint of social policy, for if these conclusions were actually adopted in practice as a law, juvenile court practice, social practice generally in relation to the custody, care, and treatment of children, and, of course, procedures intended to safeguard the rights of mentally ill persons, would be fundamentally changed. Appropriate provisions with respect to guardians and their compensation would be inserted in socio-economic laws.

Take, for example, the whole area of probationary discharges from mental institutions. All sorts of devices have been attempted in the endeavor to maintain certain essentially basic controls while giving the individual general freedom of action to test his ability to navigate for himself. The individual who is sent back to the local community needs for a while at least some supervisory care which combines knowledge of the dangers to which he is subject and of the conditions that he must face. In this situation he may also need assistance in the management of economic aids such as are available, for example, under the social security system. Guardianship in this situation, as in others, is not a professional function. It is a personal relationship that should be undertaken, if at all, under legally defined responsibilities set forth either in statute or in individual letters of guardianship. The guardian may need particularized knowledge of his ward's condition but does not have to be a doctor.

Somewhat the same considerations are applicable to the probationary placement of children. The present system, under which agency staff members make periodic visits to homes in which children have been placed for purposes of foster care and in which the agency staff is given a semi-professional and semi-authoritative role in relation to handling the child, presents a highly confused picture and certainly furnishes no underlying basis of security for the child. In fact, it is another example of the confusion that prevails throughout all applied social science today—the confusion between the authoritative and the professional roles. One simply cannot occupy both roles at the same time any more than one can serve God and Mammon at the same time. The allegiance to one theory or function militates against the other.

The values that adhere in one principle must always compete with others. The test of any guiding maxim comes always at the pinch, when adherence to it impedes or prejudices some other aim or objective. For example, we discover new solutions for individual problems, new techniques and processes of treatment, and we find ourselves at times perturbed by the unwillingness of the individual to accept the procedures that are laid out for his welfare. It may be heartrending to know that one is in position greatly to alleviate or facilitate the life of another but cannot dominate that life sufficiently to undertake it. But something far more important and precious to society will be sacrificed if the necessary authority is given without the kind of responsibility and safeguards that the institution of private guardianship requires.

There is real reason for the poignant appeal of such a letter as was written by Judge Woodward of California in explanation of his denial of an application made to him by a social agency to remove a child from its mother, its natural guardian, and commit it to an institution for the specific purpose of shifting responsibility for the treatment decision to a public authority.[3] But unless that mother and child can be made to adopt voluntarily the program laid out for them, the imme-

3. *American Journal of Public Health and the Nation's Health,* vol. 34, no. 5 (May, 1944), pp. 532-34.

diate objective will be achieved at the cost of a permanent value for which even individual life might on occasion be appropriately sacrificed. The individual's point of view must be firmly protected against the dominating strengths of the organized forces of society.

If my foster child refuses to go to school, I can put my arms around him and tell him I love him; I can work over him, climbing the stairs to his bedroom again and again, and if I win, I can start him off to school and he will go there and study, but if I attempt a short cut, or if my wife exerts upon him the great force of her irresistible will, he will seize the first avenue of escape, and the teacher will report later that Charles did not attend school that day.

Situations must inevitably and constantly occur in which apparent good will be left undone if the solution must wait upon its voluntary acceptance; yet if the will of individuals is to be preserved, society must yield its force and place its faith in the provision of a passive legal pattern in relation to which, with such guidance and help as can be given on a professional basis, the individuals concerned can build or rebuild their own lives and assume responsibility for their own salvation.

In the judiciary, and in the judiciary alone, can we hope to establish the necessary consideration for fundamental rights and prerogatives of the individual in harmony with the conditions which the social order requires. It should always be remembered that the chief concern of the law is to see to it that every opportunity is afforded for the expression of the individual's situation and point of view and the preservation of his liberties under social pressures. No executive agency can maintain this independence of view. Its loyalties and its responsibility for the techniques of treatment for which it exists condition its approach to the individual.

145

CONCLUSIONS

It will now be seen that the institution of guardianship describes a relationship with stated rights and responsibilities, a relationship that is independent of custody but controls custody. In other words, just as one's title to property is an intangible concept reflected in a deed, with rights and responsibilities entirely distinct and apart from the mere concept of possession, so guardianship places the emphasis upon these incidents of relationship and not upon the mere physical custody of another human being.

It is quite true that the actual adoption of a child, if it is a desirable adoption, is a firm substitute for the parental relationship. The guardianship relation, being more flexible, may be required as a condition to the receipt of custody of any child even though it may ultimately be necessary to make a further change in the child's status. Temporary placement under judicial auspices will furnish an appropriate basis for evaluating the relationship.

Of course no criticism is implied of the procedure whereby the child may with the consent of its parent or guardian be placed temporarily in an institution or other environment for temporary treatment purposes. There is a fundamental distinction between basic living arrangements and treatment. But no child should be without a parent by blood or operation of law at any time. His status should be a continuing fact that insures his personal security, his power of expression, and representation, a fact that gives him, in other words, a legal personality.

This leads us to consider what the role of the court should be and what changes of primary significance are necessary in law and practice. The needed changes relate much more to procedure than to the substance of the law. This legal institution, ancient and well defined, needs most of all at this juncture to be invoked and used. If I were a judge, I should not want to assume responsibility for "committing" any child or any allegedly incompetent adult to a public department or agency, training school or institution, without first inquiring into the individual's guardianship and doing whatever was needed to cure its defects. I should want to see that society had made up for any default of its own in this regard. If the individual had to be "committed" somewhere, either to prevent him from doing some harm to society or for purposes of corrective treatment, I should want all the more on this account to make sure that he had an appropriate private guardian.

While it has been pointed out that court and agency resources would be disastrously overtaxed by an immediately effective mandate which would require that a guardian be appointed for every child without a parent and for every incompetent adult who needed it, there is nevertheless need for a positive legislative declaration which would establish the responsibility of society for securing the individual's legal representation and establishing his right to a definite legal status, not only before any court, but whenever his custody is assumed by a public agency or private family, unless, perhaps, the latter situation is a very temporary expedient. The law should provide for the assumption of child custody to be assumed on a legally responsible basis in all cases, as a means of effecting secure and responsible relationships. Effectuation of these points of policy should insure simple procedure and implementation of the court to enable it to exercise its more extensive responsibilities.

The failure to envisage private guardianship as an operative system in society stems very largely from conceptions of the inflexibility of judicial procedure, and hence, of its inconsistency with the kind of freedom that modern technicians in fields of human reconstruction demand for the exercise of their skills. There is consequently need for much more flexible judicial procedure, especially as regards the appointment of guardians on a temporary basis, if judicial procedures are not going to continue to yield to administrative techniques.

As applied to adult guardianship there is an analogous need for the appointment of types of special guardians to provide protection and service to types of mentally ill individuals without branding the individual as incompetent as that term is now legally defined, and without depriving him of those civil rights which he can still intelligently exercise of his own volition. As the knowledge of mental illness is extended, it becomes possible to carve out those areas in which the individual's will and its expression is affected to such an extent as to render him incapable of anything approaching an objective decision, and hence in need of personality supplementation. The author is advised that, in the drafting of the Act, above mentioned, to govern hospitalization of the mentally ill, the effect of branding the individual as incompetent strongly influenced the draftsmen.

There is a basic need, also, for developing technical staffs, routinized reporting procedures, and other machinery essential to the performance of the court's more intensive responsibilities. Special emphasis needs to be placed on non-fiscal phases of guardianship accounting.

Care should, however, be taken to see that the court is not turned into an administrative or supervisory agency. One would not care to see the juvenile court assume the functions of welfare departments or agencies or involve itself in the processes of home finding, of social investigations, and all the other administrative operations carried on by child welfare agencies. In guardianship, I am concerned with the incidence of authority in human relationships, not with the functions of those who minister professionally to them. The court, itself, does not properly make decisions for individuals unless under necessity. Its function is to give the individual the means of decision and to safeguard the individual and insure the efficacy of his prerogatives.

Care should also be taken to see, for example, that, in the enlargement of its facilities for fact finding, this judicial function is conducted by methods that have been found throughout the ages to be the most reliable means for establishing the truth. In our zeal for making courts more socially minded, judicial traditions and strengths must be preserved. Judicial relationships with public and private social agencies, for example, should be founded upon the fact that the interested agency is a party in the proceedings. On this basis they will be expected to furnish disinterested witnesses. The facts and advice which welfare agencies have to give should thus be subjected to the test of judicial scrutiny before it is applied to human beings.

However, it is clear that the courts, under present methods and conditions, are quite incapable of assuming the responsibility that this program imposes upon them for the *success* of the guardian-ward relationships which they sponsor. Present statutes are often designed to enable the courts to avoid this responsibility rather than to assume it. There are, for example, the rigid eligibility provisions that may govern the appointment of a guardian. Often a more or less rigid system of eligibility priorities is created by statute. In addition, the court is not prepared to satisfy itself as to the qualifications of the guardian or assure itself that the individual's particular need will be served. The court has become accustomed to rely on oaths and surety bonds whose function is to save the ward from monetary loss. These have very little value in personal guardianship situations. This, together with the similar inconsistency of relying upon purely perfunctory reports and accounting in such cases, bespeaks the need for a court equipped to procure the facts and deal with the merits of the proposed relationships.

We have been talking, of course, in terms of personal guardianship. For whatever reason, the property guardian has over the years encroached upon realms sacred to the personal guardian. Recognition of the importance of the functions of personal guardianship today and its reinstatement as a social institution and welfare institution would naturally lead to a reinstatement of the broader boundaries of personal guardianship. Property guardianship is appropriately limited to property management. Such is the practical importance of using a financial institution. Property guardianship should not, for example, extend to the expenditure of a maintenance income, because participation in the expenditure of an individual's maintenance income involves responsibility for the intimate activities of his daily life. He who has responsibility for the expenditure of the ward's $40 to $50 per month, has responsibility for the very life of the ward. This is the function of a personal guardian. This is an important consideration in view of the wide incidence of Social Security payments, veterans' benefits, health benefits, and similar payments. We need responsible, private, personal guardianship. Perhaps nothing illustrates more vividly the early shift of law toward purely technical and economic considerations than the provision for depositing small sums (usually not exceeding $300 or $500) with the clerk of the court, providing thereby a legal means of acquittance, but avoiding all responsibility for the recipient and his employment of the money.

The sixty-four-dollar question that is always propounded at this point is, "Where do we get guardians?" One answer is that we will have guardians where we now have persons acting in a guardianship capacity but without acknowledging their responsibilities. I think, however, that private guardianship cannot be supplied gratis. No doubt there are values not translatable into dollars and cents. The love and sacrifice of a parent is of this order—but that does not prove that personal as well as property guardians should not be compensated from the "ward's estate" for the time and effort they in fact and of necessity bestow upon the welfare of their charges and in the representation of them and in accounting for what they do. The belief shared by many that personal guardians should not be paid stems largely from the inadequacies of the present system and the failure to envisage effective methods of insuring an awakened sense of guardianship responsibility.

But to secure payment of guardianship costs from the estate of the ward, the ward must have an estate. This implies, among other things, that social security and all other payments intended to provide the individual with the basic maintenance income must include the reasonable costs of guardianship whensoever guardians may be appointed. The legal right of the ward to such payments must be of such a character as to make it clear that the guardian derives his compensation from the ward. Guardians cannot be supplied as a cost of government or as an administrative cost of some social agency, public or private, without destroying the very values that this legal institution was made to supply. He who pays the piper calls the tune.

It is unfortunate, no doubt, that the needs of individuals appear more often than not in inverse ratio to their capacities. This is perhaps easier to accept understandingly in the case of children as a class than in the case of adult individuals. But modern social science has been steadily building upon its discoveries of the potentialities that lie in human beings. This is its faith—but the foundations of this faith are in essence merely a confirmation of the faith upon which the law itself builds when it insists that every individual shall stand as an equal *persona sui juris* before the law. We must be willing to pay the costs of preserving the foundations of our individualistic society.

Chapter 11

Delinquency Procedures

Every mental foray that I have undertaken to analyze social programs has sharply emphasized for me the significance of the concepts of legal guardianship. Take, for example, the juvenile court and its surrounding systems of probation, institutional training, and family placement. What I propose to show is that the whole system, with its judicial concentration, is or should be a study in the law and practice of guardianship.

It has been stated frequently, and correctly, that the juvenile court stemmed basically from the need for separate trials of children charged with crime. At common law children between seven and fourteen years of age might, or might not, be held to have a responsibility in the criminal sense for their acts. A baby may pluck out your eye and do it with a very hostile intent, but he cannot be held to have committed a criminal act. He lacks the controls over his actions which must be present before the individual can be held answerable under the criminal law.

The same theory which holds that the child is not on trial within the criminal jurisdiction, however, renders unavailable to him basic constitutional safeguards found necessary to insure the just treatment of adults charged with unsocial behavior. The difficulty is that we have failed so completely to abolish punishment concepts and sanctions in juvenile cases that what is done to a child in the name of treatment may be quite indistinguishable from the treatment accorded an adult —or differ from it mainly in the fact that it may continue for years in cases where an adult would have been released with a reprimand. I wonder sometimes if the child's behavior may not often have had even less significance than the adult's behavior. For example, as I write these words, I have just come from a juvenile court proceeding in which a boy was present in response to a summons served on him for crossing the double line at the center of a highway. This he did in passing another vehicle. The arresting officer had made it quite clear that no further circumstance, such as excessive speeding, was present to prejudice the case. Since it was a first offense, an adult might well have gone scot free. The juvenile court judge, exercising his free and unrestrained jurisdiction and assuming himself to be a sufficient psychologist to do so, questioned the boy at length about many things and having confused him sufficiently to elicit a very tactless comment, ended by suspending his operator's license for six months. Such an experience will never be forgotten, and causes me to wonder how I may best preserve the regard and respect of "my boy" (I am presently a sponsor), for the institutions of society!

In fact it happens in some cases that the boy's very youth may prolong the "sentence." This may happen, for example, in cases where it is a matter of custom or habit to commit the boy for the remainder of his minority. The varying policies of the federal courts in the enforcement of the act which authorizes commitment of any child who takes an automobile across a state line, "knowing the same to have been stolen," [1] is another example. (I am not the only one who would like

---

1. See Dyer Act, U.S.C.A., Tit. 18, § 2312.

to see some old cars placed in municipal lots and reserved exclusively for joy rides, subject, of course, to whatever safe-guards may be found necessary to protect life and property.)

The prime difficulty is that our juvenile court philosophy is warped by an unfortunate misconception of the procedures and practice of the English Chancery Court, to which juvenile court procedure is presumed to be related in many aspects. This misconception is symbolized in the phrase "ward of the court." The significance which this phrase has acquired and the practices that have resulted, seem to have arisen in the main from the notion that English Masters in Chancery actu-ally acted as guardians of the children referred to them—in other words, the notion has been spread that infants were directly under the control and supervision of Chancery. This notion probably arose from the belief that the infancy juris-diction of the Equity Court could be traced historically to the function of the Chancellor as an administrative officer.[2] Chancellors had administrative responsibilities in early times. They will be remembered as the Keepers of the King's Con-science. But the better view is that the jurisdiction of the English Chancery Court in respect of infants originated not as an administrative but as a purely judicial function. It was exercised within the approved concepts governing judicial procedure in the appointment of guardians. The purpose in most cases was to provide for the custody and management of the child's estate. More than any other single influence, how-ever, this concept of the child as a "ward of the court" has helped to spread the notion that the juvenile court should adopt the manners and functions of an administrative agency.

The judicial function is not, of course, to adopt wards but to create guardians. The court institutes guardian-ward re-

2. John Norton Pomeroy, *Treatise on Equity Jurisprudence* ... (San Fran-cisco, Bancroft, 5th ed.), Vol. IV, § 1304.

lationships. The court does not itself act as a guardian but appoints guardians.

The *parens patriae* doctrine is commonly referred to in this connection. But the *parens patriae* doctrine, upon which the guardianship jurisdiction of the court basically depends, also supports nearly all public welfare undertakings of society. Of course, nothing could be further from the truth than the notion that the *parens patriae* theorem means that the state is a parent or can properly function as a parent. In fact, the phrase does not sponsor any particular method of social action. It is a very basic constitutional theorem which underlies most of our modern social programs. It is not paternalistic or administrative, but legal and judicial, in its connotations. Far from authorizing the state to act as a parent, it merely assigns it the responsibility for seeing that children are parented by operation of law. For this purpose the court can appoint substitute parents or guardians and may act thereafter as a point of reference when the relationship requires the intervention of a court for the resolution of doubts and conflicts.

The juvenile court, however, is in no sense a criminal court. Its jurisdiction, properly conceived, springs from the child's need of adequate guardianship to assure the meeting of individual needs. Infancy, with its presumed lack of criminal responsibility, is the basis of its jurisdiction. As a civil guardianship court, it is free to delve into the motivations of child behavior unencumbered by concepts of criminality—except, of course, for the fact that we are all encumbered in our thinking by concepts of criminality.[3]

---

3. This paragraph could appropriately be supported by a long list of judicial pronouncements. But such is not the purpose of this book. What I seek here is basic orientation, and the kind of matured thought which will read the texts affecting juvenile court theory with a more critical discernment than that which has prompted unthinking repetition of traditions that are not historically supportable and dogmas that are not legally scientific.

An infant is a person *non sui juris*. The perfection of a child's legal personality, as we have seen, postulates a guardian. In practice it would appear that the juvenile court is inquiring into the sufficiency of the existing guardianship of the child and may, if dissatisfied with what its investigation turns up, do one of two things: either appoint a new private guardian temporarily or permanently, or superimpose public guardianship controls (as, for example, in the use of probation) or a public guardian upon the private parental or guardian relationship in the social interest. In the latter case, it is, of course, invoking the police power.

But, of course, juvenile court statutes existing at the time of this writing make the court's jurisdiction turn upon findings of delinquency and also, often, on findings of social dependency and neglect. The definitions of delinquency and dependency in some statutes are so broad that, when literally read, children become delinquent whenever they eat in restaurants that are licensed to sell wine and beer to adult customers. This is thought necessary to give the court authority to proceed wherever its authority seems needed. If, however, the court's procedures were grounded merely on a showing that a question of suitable guardianship or of custody was involved, and if the governing statute so provided, these all-embracing statutory definitions of delinquency and dependency would be quite unnecessary and inappropriate.

Now, as we have seen, the private guardian and the public guardian protect primarily two very different interests—one, that of the individual; the other, that of society. The interest of society demands protection, for example, of such mundane things as the property and property rights of its members. The child's individual interest demands an environment that affords opportunity for the pursuit of his basic drives as they develop. It is futile to say that these two interests are not presently in conflict when a child is taken into custody and declared to

157

be a delinquent, even though ultimately the two interests may be reconciled and perhaps harmonized. Otherwise we but restate the same fallacy reflected in the remark of a court clerk that Mr. X's imprisonment raised no question of conflicting interest, since X's own welfare will be advanced if he is put in jail. It is said that X merely proves his perversity when he does not accept this fact.

The harmonization of these two interests grows out of their mutual expression in a judicial tribunal. That's why we have courts. So far as possible, action should be taken to protect both interests, though it is difficult to take issue with one who asserts that the immediate social interest must be protected in any event.

I think that an understanding of the conflict between public interest and private interest, and the means of its reconciliation, are manifest only when you visualize the whole proceeding as a guardianship procedure. The private guardian's interest embraces the entire life of the individual, past, present, and future. The social interest reflects the immediate concerns of society and the interests of the individuals who compose it, those, I mean, who may be affected by the action of the ward. The two interests, society's and the child's, are reconcilable only as you raise your sights from the present to the ultimate future. It is the immediate practical situation that points up the conflict.

However, as we proceed with this guardianship study, it seems clear that public guardianship in the social interest, resting as all agree in the police power, is, as is most police power action, a temporary surveillance or public control and a mere modifying factor in the overall concerns of the individual. The public guardian appointed by reason of the child's anti-social behavior has, therefore, a far more limited function in its own right, a far more limited purview for the protection of its own interests, than has the child's private guardian, be he parent or substitute parent. This rather obvious truth forces the conclusion that remedial and rehabilitative action designed to benefit the individual child requires the participation of the child's private guardian or parent since it is in the entire context of the child's life that this remedial action must be taken.

This is the central problem, or at least a key to the central problem, in the whole proceeding. This need is the chief support for the conviction that "no child should be institutionalized without having a parent or guardian concerned with his welfare and with his treatment" during the period of institutionalization. This is a conclusion founded on philosophical and ethical grounds, as well as on legal and social principles. At the present time, however, children who are removed from their parental homes, or existing private guardianship, as delinquent children, have in most instances no private or parental guardianship during the period of their institutionalization. In fact the general theory seems to be that, since parental supervision has failed, public supervision should be substituted. Or rather, it is said, the child needs a course of treatment.

Furthermore, it so happens today that when a child is sent to a training school the sentinels of the child's private, personal life abruptly cease to function. Whatever disciplines were operative in the private life of the child are suddenly forsaken; nor, save in rare instances, can it be said that other disciplines are substituted; for, as every soldier knows and as the institutionalized child unconsciously observes, individuals normally lose rather than add to their sense of personal responsibility when they live under close supervision. Any soldier, newly recruited, placed in a troop train with guards at either end will have experienced this sudden sense of the loss of responsibility for his own life and behavior. There is a sudden letdown in controls, a release of pressure, and an abandonment of concern.

In this comment I do not for a moment lose sight of the significance of the "need to belong" and of the other basic values in home and friends. Rather I am pointing out that in the treatment process there is need to incorporate and build upon these values, instincts, and relationships. The need for the disciplines of private life, using this word "disciplines" in the broadest sense, is good reason for preferring private placement to institutionalization in most situations. For them no public guardian can provide a substitute; nor, as every lawyer knows, can this divergency of public and private wills and interests be placed in the keeping of the same individual. His actions will inevitably be motivated by those ends that command his first allegiance. More than anything else you need today to re-enforce and implement the private, the individual interests of the child. Group treatment alone cannot effectuate these interests. So often they are merely suppressed, disciplined perhaps, to the point of extinction. It should be recalled that aggressiveness is not in and of itself delinquency.

The National Training School at Washington, with its present "voluntary sponsor" program, and other institutions which have attempted to establish some sort of sponsorship, "Big Brother," or "outside friend" program, have acted generally in the awareness of this need. But the lay sponsor or friend in these experiments has no authority and no commitment. He acts as counsellor, friend, and advocate. The child's need is for a parent, since after all he is an infant. The parent or guardian should stand between the boy and all professional counsellors. The counselling of a child oversteps the professional role. It involves an element of supervision. The boy's guardian, rather than the boy, is the one through whom professional advice and advocacy are appropriately applied.

The ultimate test of a sponsorship program will be found in

its effect upon recidivism. My present personal experience with this problem indicates that while many institutions are doing a fairly good job in cases that warranted institutionalization, and while a good deal of effective work is being done by professional advisers in the operative field, the breakdown, the heart-rending breakdown, comes when the child is sought to be restored to communal life. Under present practices these institutionalized relationships often provide merely one more occasion for a traumatic experience when the boy is paroled. Some "sponsors" attempt to place the child or get him a job. I understand that in a few cases the sponsor of an institutionalized boy has succeeded in delegating or transferring his role to someone in the child's locale upon his release from the institution, but the very possibility of this minimizes one's conception of the role which the sponsor or friend had been fulfilling in the institutional life of the child.

But let us return to the main organizational problem, and see now what solutions are suggested when we visualize the whole process as a guardianship proceeding and procedure.

Both public and private guardian-ward relationships are, of course, authoritative—all guardianship is authoritative. To place a child, that is, to commit a child—to use police power language—to a welfare department for the purposes of its public guardianship is, therefore, one example of glaring inconsistency in present welfare practice. A welfare department appropriately eschews such authoritative roles and wisely conceives itself as a professional servicing agency. Public guardianship of a child is incompatible with this conception of its functioning, even if its guardianship concerns were restricted to reflect the public interest solely—which they never would be, since modern theory demands the right to treat the child "as a whole."

The juvenile court and the training system associated with it are at the present time in a state of development analogous to that of the automobile while it continued to resemble the carriage from which it emerged. The carriage in this instance symbolizes the criminal dress wherein alone all unsocial behavior was formerly conceived. Taking the child out of the custody and control of his natural parents was also conceived as a part of the criminal proceeding. All recent cases hold, however, that the parents are entitled, as a matter of due process (and therefore as a matter of constitutional right), to a formal hearing on the issue of their right to custody. This underlines the truth that the whole procedure should be viewed in its proper guardianship context. The hearing, with its determination of the issue as to whether or not the child is to be taken from the custody of its parents, is then properly viewed as a hearing on the adequacy of the parent qua guardian. The parental custody is challenged from the standpoint of the due performance of its guardianship responsibilities.

The court's so-called "continuing jurisdiction" is also properly identified as that which appertains to any guardianship court which either appoints a substitute guardian, that is, a substitute parent, or subjects the child to temporary public supervision, that is, public guardianship, or public surveillance. The court in such cases remains open to hear all reports and petitions affecting the guardianship relationships which it has instituted. The professional role, moreover, continues in its normal functioning as adviser to the public custodian as well as to the private guardian appointee, and the guardian having custody, whether acting in the private or public interest, subjects himself to the usual judicial procedure in guardianship cases. I refer not only to the accounting responsibility imposed on a guardian, but to the guardian's submission of unusual decisions to the court for resolution. The guardianship court should pass on all questions of major significance, including proposals involving a physical or health hazard as well as any

162

disposition vitally affecting the child's future. The professional service yields its authoritative assignments, but is required, as we all are properly required, to prove the wisdom and worth of its advice and of its analyses before an adjudicatory tribunal. Lawyers take this responsibility for granted. So should social workers.

Responsibility for the public surveillance of the child should, of course, be centered in an agency; but, as we have just seen, a basic change of plan or program with respect to the child should be referred to the court for confirmation or validation. Our analysis, moreover, shows also that where public guardianship in the social interest is necessary, the appointee should occupy a central position with respect to the home, court, and professional agencies concerned. Most important of all: it should be in a position, as has been shown, to incorporate the child's private, personal, individual concerns in its treatment processes. But a court does not properly seek to manage or supervise the actual activities of an individual. It does not properly do so even when it appoints a guardian. It should not seek to employ the guardian as its mere ministerial agent. This is wrong both because it turns the court into an administrative agency and also because it is wrong for an administrative agency to do so. When we turn a judicial agency into an administrative agency, we sacrifice the judicial values. We lose sight of the basic reason for courts. We forfeit the very safeguards that reference to the court was intended to insure. Basically there is a disregard of the most significant of all constitutional safeguards—I refer to the division of powers—legislative, executive, and judicial. Those prohibitions and procedures that are essential to safeguard our freedom, are different in each case.

Probation is not a judicial function. Experience teaches that this probation service, especially when it undertakes to "supervise" the periods of parole, may come into grievous conflict with those responsible for the "plan," in other words, with the child's guardians, including at present, of course, the training school or the welfare department in a guardianship role. The probation officer is able, upon occasion, to veto plans worked out for the future upbringing of the child. He may do this by refusing to "supervise" the parolee on the ground that the plan is impractical.

As I said, the court itself is properly called upon to approve a new guardian or to approve a fundamental plan for the child by its guardian, or it may be to arbitrate differences between the private guardian and public custodian, let us say, upon the termination of a period of institutionalization.

The judicial function is called into action only when it is needed. It acts upon that which is presented to it—and it generally acts to resolve the problem referred to it by a single act or pronouncement. It does not "take over," to use the common phrase. It stands ready to act in cases where authority or protection is needed. Responsibility for treatment proposals properly rests, therefore, with the guardian, be he public or private. In behavior cases, where some immediate interest of society is harmed or threatened, this responsibility for proposing a plan of treatment centers in the public guardian. For this purpose a strong, mobile agency is needed with ability to work in cooperation with all of the interests and facilities that may be involved.

Some of this philosophy, no doubt, is inherent in the conception of a youth authority at the present time. Probably the most important element in this whole conception of concentric and interrelated action is the relationship of this authority to the private guardian, parent, or other home of the child. Take, for example, the National Training School in Washington. This school receives children from all states as well as from the District of Columbia. Thus, there are really two groups of children involved. The national group are there because of having crossed a state line, probably in an automobile appropriated for the occasion, or perhaps because of having entered upon federal property. These children are definitely cut off from home. Large numbers of them have not seen any relative for perhaps a year or more. Then, after a year or so, they are suddenly released to the community which repudiated them originally; a community in which they may have built up for themselves a very unsavory reputation, and where the school did little for them except to certify, perhaps quite unjustifiably, their passage from year to year to a higher grade. For example, I asked a boy who was in the eighth grade at the time he was sent to the training school, how much 8 x 9 is and he started off with 99 and gave me various other suggestions. In the meantime, the father and step-mother of such a boy will have added to the size of their family and the general problem of family surveillance will have gotten more or less out of hand. The home life of the boy had already become rather "messed up" when he fell into the hands of the "law"!

The most faithful "sponsor" of such a boy at the National Training School told me that out of nine boys he had successfully sponsored, five, no fewer than five, had been returned to institutions upon their parole by the National Training School. This particular sponsor had endeavored to do what he could, travelling all the way to Texas in one case in a trying situation.

"My boy" would quite possibly step into the same future if the proposal of the probation officer to have him sent back to "school" in the community were allowed to prevail. The situation is so perfectly obvious, the terrifying figures are so perfectly understandable, that I could never have thought of "sponsoring" a boy and of then stepping aside to see any such thing occur. I propose to be a real personal guardian and see the problem through. I began by restoring family and community ties at once. I re-established the lane of communication between this boy and his youthful sweetheart in his home community (he is mature at sixteen). I brought his brother on to Washington to see him. I kept his father promptly advised of all developments in the boy's institutional career. However, I can see no method of continuing this development at a distance of four or five hundred miles, so in this particular instance I would propose to have the boy exchange his father for me and see what the correction of the weaknesses and deprivations in his life will achieve. In other words, I invited the boy to share my home. May he not someday do something more than I can about the problems of those who have shared his deprivations and his troubles?

I have presented this illustration to make it clear that the obvious fallacies, today, are not so much in corrective treatment, some forms of which have been deeply considered and wisely undertaken, but in the idea that you can suddenly put a boy in an institutional hospital for behavior abnormalities, cure him, and send him back as though it were a case of tuberculosis or a severed artery. Obviously there is needed an arm whose fingers reach into every facet of the situation, and a mind which at the very least is capable of relating the public to the private action, and recognizes that the public's intervention is of an emergency character, and that its interests are best subserved when the private interest is best subserved. In other words, to solve the child's problem you must possess the knowledge that can be acquired only by one who has seen his reactions in his intimate life over a period of time and then you must apply that knowledge in the dispositions that you make for the purpose of starting him on a course of life.

One may not study this picture for any length of time without realizing that he must be prepared to face every quirk and distortion of human life. While at the moment more than ninety per cent of the state boys in the National Training School have been on a joy ride, and while an inquiry from one boy or another will bring forth the fact that his mother has died, that his father has remarried, or will indicate some other frustrated need, comprehended in the word "rejection," it is plain that every mental ailment or physical ailment, every pattern of family disruption, in short every broken thread in the web of human life, is represented. One needs to appreciate that fact when he seeks to paint an appropriate legal pattern. This immediately carries one back to the established pattern of private guardianship procedure with its continuing unbroken personal relationship operating in the context of public controls. It is a pattern familiar to the law because the law mirrors every facet of human life. It appoints a guardian as God appoints a parent. But, dressed as always in its judicial robes, it must dominate the picture where harmonization of conflicting interests is required. This is the essential teaching of human history.

Furthermore you need, in the light of history, to make no apology for the judicial arm. One human being cannot in a society that calls itself free be entrusted with the life of another or be placed in control of another except under judicial auspices. Managing the lives of individuals is not appropriately an executive function. That, indeed, is the answer to any apologist for dictatorship. Whether the interests which you subserve, or in support of which you act, are public or private, the mere fact that you act in a guardianship capacity is complete justification for keeping a judicial robe in effective control of the operation. In other words, all guardianship action must be undertaken upon the understanding that it is subject to be passed upon by the judiciary. It is never sufficient to constitute a guardianship court merely as a tribunal of appeal unless it is a tribunal of appeal only in the sense that there are actively functioning guardians whose referral of significant issues to the court is automatic and independent of an infant's action. You can hardly expect an infant to initiate personally action for the protection of his rights. An infant knows only enough to appeal to his fists or to his guardian.

LAW IN THE TREATMENT PROCESS

Up to this point my analysis has dealt with the over-all administrative and judicial pattern, but the whole point of these chapters is missed if it be considered that legal science stops here and does not enter into the treatment process. I would not fear the consequences of dumping one of these institutionalized young people back into the community that spewed him forth, if he had learned in the interim to follow rules in the absence of a policeman. The idea that a child has been rehabilitated by being placed for a limited period under personal surveillance, and by accommodating himself to such a security regime, seems ridiculous. He was institutionalized because, living in a free community and reaching an age when he became mobile and anxious to look about and see the world, he scorned for the nonce family and community controls and ordinances. In short, he was institutionalized because he had not learned to rule himself. To punish him and then send him back to his community, though in a chastened mood, is a naive procedure. What is now done for the most part is done under the gospel of the past, which preached salvation through punishment. What is now done is not consonant with the theorem of training and rehabilitation.

But my prescriptions require an understanding of what law is. Few do understand what law really is. At the moment the lessened regard for law attests the common misapprehension of law. Law and social controls are two different things. Law as we have seen, is law in so far as it operates to determine the consequences of action. To live under the rule of law, therefore, means that you accept the consequences of your acts which law decrees and in fact reach your goals by understanding the relation of a rule to your own acts and so, by using the rules, you achieve your aims. Therefore, if I were running a training institution, I should endeavor to see that every child in it was, as rapidly as was feasible, placed in some situation which he could control and was provided with an objective he fully understood and could easily achieve. The resulting action in the achievement of such an objective is the beginning of responsibility. It would not matter at first how unimportant the aim or function might be. However, I would endeavor as far as possible to see that nothing save the child's own action controlled the result. I would try to see that at every turn he faced the effects of his acts and understood what was, is, and might have been in those terms. He would thus be taught to face and accept the consequences. The teaching would be simple and unmistakable.

I am fully confirmed in the view that evocation of a sense of personal responsibility is the major goal of the treatment process. And this is acquired, and I firmly believe can only be acquired, by operating in an environment ruled by ethical law.

Gradually, then, I would try to make the child see the operation of law on the ethical and moral plane. I would show him the effects of his action in terms of other people, ultimately in terms of the suffering of those who put their trust in him. We cannot overlook the fact that the effects of vicarious suffering are observable only at the moral level and hence only in the sight of one who is human enough to be a moral being. In the absence of the moral sense, sacrifice is meaningless. An animal without any moral perception is unresponsive and unreachable even at the foot of the cross. It takes ages to create a moral sense, but nearly all human beings now possess it, at least in embryo. This being so, it is within the competence of human beings to sharpen its perceptions.

In short, I would see that when my boy was paroled, he had graduated from a course of training which offered some assurance of his ability to apply the simplest abstract rules of ethical behavior to his own life, to live by rule and not merely by dictation. Until he can do this, he is not prepared to run on his own and will, therefore, soon wind up in a second wreck.

Chapter 12

THE PROFESSIONAL IDEA

Modern social science stands sponsor for the professional idea. Because its purpose is to find positive and efficacious ways to achieve its objectives, it rejects the methods of the police power.

The police power may be used to prohibit and stamp out activities that are harmful. It opposes will with organized and determined will. It is a weapon usable against strength. It is of no avail to combat weakness. In the main, social science is concerned with creating strengths not with suppressing them. Its hope of success is destroyed whenever it is made a tool of the police power. Social science and the police power do not mix.

The police power orders children off the streets. It prohibits the employment of children in mines or in other occupations harmful to growth. It prohibits their living in dangerous and unsanitary dwellings. It outlaws institutional standards below the pale of decency and health. It may be used to remove children, and in some cases adults, from an environment or guardianship that harms them. It removes perverted or delinquent individuals from society. All this is important, you say.

But these are all behavior problems that ought not to exist. The police power does not strike at their causes and hence cannot end them. The use of the police power creates conditions that require its continued use. The professional idea in modern society approaches these situations from a direction precisely opposite, diametrically opposite, to that taken by the police power.

The professional idea is positive. It involves the proposal to "ride along with" or "run with" the individual in the knowledge that he possesses at base a vital force which, freed as far as possible from whatever blocks or distorts its functioning, is by its very nature or definition a constructive agent. The professional idea proposes to strengthen the capacities of the will of the individual to realize his best goals. It proposes to implement and make constructive use of parental aspirations. It proposes to enable individuals to purchase shelter that meets basic standards of health and decency. It proposes to enable mothers to keep their children when lack of money would cause their abandonment. It proposes, for example, to eliminate the economic motif from state laws that waste the skills of professionally trained personnel by employing them to decide which state has the primary monetary obligation for an abandoned child. It proposes to provide trained guardians and to see that adoptions are motivated by a concern for the child. It proposes to maintain health in preference to curing illness. In rehabilitation, it proposes to build upon whatever capacity and compensating strengths it finds within the individual himself. It proposes to assure the individual of his ability to make higher ground.

All of these things involve substituting individual rights for police power prohibitions. They invoke the tax power for a more constructive and lasting purpose than the police power can attain. They are motivated by the conviction that policing can merely eliminate the worst; but manifests no power to elevate. The police power is a blood-letting rather than a blood-supplying process.

For this reason it is disconcerting to recall that laws passed to promote the welfare of society grew up and became an authentic function of government, because they were viewed as an exercise of the general police power. But this simply means that the way we think about government and the way we use government in our effort to improve social conditions must change. The police power is not a creative technic. Human society is something we must create, or construct.

The professional idea is seeking to convert weakness into strength. It is proving that the frustrated and defeated individual can be reactivated and that his capacity for constructive and responsible action can be stimulated when there is placed at his disposal the skill, knowledge, and strength of someone whose experience has comprehended all that the individual has been up against, and who can use his professional capacities to exalt but not to dominate him. To do this successfully is an art, for it requires getting down on the plane occupied by the individual himself, seeing his problem as he himself sees it, and then yielding him the use of greater and more specialized knowledge and capacity, while meticulously refraining from any trick or device of self-imposition. The tool that is used is the inspiring effect of intimate human relationships. One may thus yield one's blood to the heart of another and one's strength to the command of another's will. The method is a healing art of untold possibilities. The will is a dynamo. You cannot control a dynamo by opposing it but only by making yourself party to its activities. You *can* constrain the will—but never effectively by seeking to prejudice its dominance and sway, for this impugns the very essence and integrity of its function. This kills the very will that you are expecting to initiate action. You can induce ethical action only by charging the caravans that go back to the individual with an ethical reaction, one that he appreciates as being in his interest. Every great novelist who wishes to explain the transformation of a character from attitudes of vengeful hostility to consecrated service confronts him with an act of overpowering selflessness, a substitution of "you" for "me." Or if you prefer an illustration from a wholly different sphere, take the aviator in a tail-spin who finds that he can extricate himself not by opposing the force but by removing opposition, by moving with it and increasing its effect, or as you might say, by giving it more than it bargained for. The will is constrained to reciprocate ethic with ethic. You alone can commit yourself. Each individual's commitment must come from himself. This is neither practical nor impractical so it be the truth.

The individual must somehow be rid of the sense of being hemmed in by a wilful and force-minded environment. He needs no independently motivated opposition; but he needs the feel of power, the confident sense of command. He needs therefore a free-way, a medium receptive to his attack. He generally needs a sponsor to attest his demands upon the agencies of organized society. The professional idea, generally, is the individual's best bulwark to save him from being beaten down by a force-and-will-minded world. This explains the importance of being professional rather than authoritative when you proffer your services to a human being. The individual is the principal in the transaction. To serve him is not to supervise him. The professional agent should remember from first to last that his end is to aid the *will* of man to become effective, to realize its own expressive powers and capacities, and to achieve the best aims and ideals by which it may be prompted.

The professional method is slowly transforming our conception of government. As government concerns itself more and more with this positive approach to the solution of human problems, it must eventually occur to any observer that the professional method is substituting itself and must continue to substitute itself for the authoritative method in the performance of public functions. Government itself and the representatives of government thus become professional persons and professional agencies. This may seem a rather novel idea at first, to one who thinks of government as authority and its representatives as "the authorities"; but it is the logical result of concentrating on functions that serve and strengthen the life of the individual.

RELATION TO SOCIAL WORK AS A PROFESSION

Professionalism is the normal complement of a legally ruled society. We cease to be authoritative in the presence of a legal right because legal rights establish the authority of the one who successfully maintains them. He who "has the law on his side" occupies the dominant role. In order properly to fulfill our responsibilities as professional members in social programs under public auspices, we need to remain aware that we are merely servicing rights created by law. We need to see ourselves as ministrants of the law, and therefore as serving one another. We need to dedicate our capacities to such services.

This proves, of course, that members of a profession can work in some capacity in an agency which is operating public service programs without prejudice to their professional standing. They can, that is, if the client is not a mere suppliant but occupies a secure legal position. Without a clear statutory right to the service he receives, however, the individual finds himself dependent upon a discretion he cannot control—a discretion that is not properly restricted to the survey and diagnosis of facts, but extends to the recognition or rejection of claims on individual bases that are legally determinable. These considerations lead me to conclude that the staff of a private agency, engaged in the dispensation of things of material value, such as medical care, public assistance, or other

175

rehabilitative service which they are free to give or withhold in the individual case, will suffer proportionately in terms of their professional status, since they are not dealing with the agency's so-called client on a wholly professional basis. The responsibilities they assume vis-à-vis the individual are determinative and therefore authoritative.

Modern development, however, especially the spread of public social service, raises a much more acute question as to the professional status of social work in view of the organizational patterns within the agency and in view of the relations between social work and other disciplines. It had never occurred to me to question the professional claim in these terms until I saw social workers operating within, and in the higher echelons of the chain of command in public agencies, where they controlled the use and the services of other professions, including both law and medicine. I believe that this fact explains some of the acrimony that has accompanied consideration of the relation between social work and the other professions. Social work has been conceived in the light of this development as an instrumentality for corralling other professional skills and disciplines and for directing their application. The social worker who possesses a special competence in his or her ability to deal with people will be assigned responsibility by reason thereof for coordinating the skills of others at least, it is said, in relation to the lower economic strata of our society. The social worker becomes a kind of professional supervisor. This approach suggests further, in view of their managerial responsibilities and the responsibilities they assume with respect to their clients, that social workers become a kind of guardianship reservoir, or a source of supply for parole and probation officers.

Social workers are not the only ones who suffer from this blight. Doctors and lawyers who take executive jobs, superimpose an authoritative function on their professional status.

The Professional Idea

There are those, however, who think that a lawyer is still a functioning lawyer when he is in fact presiding over a corporation and that a doctor is still a professional physician when he is directing an institution. But the fundamental fact is that managing or supervising people is a highly executive function. It is not a professional job.

It seems to me that as we become less authoritative and more responsive to law, we shall come to define more narrowly the executive or managerial function in any agency. It is not for the acting executive, I think, to make policy but to derive policy formulations from the operations of the professional disciplines within the agency. The professional staff should develop agency position and draft the agency's texts.

No doubt social work is misconceived because of its institutional involvement, but this would be as true of any other profession. It takes a broad background of private practice to dispel the illusions one gets from seeing the function only in institutional dress; for it is in the broad fields of private practice that a profession builds the sure foundations of its professional ethic and discovers also the empirical answers to the sixty-four-dollar question as to what course of action its ethical standards require. Social work has suffered even more, in my estimation, from the necessity under which it operates, of acting as the guardian of individuals, a function it often fulfills without appointment. All these extra-curriculum activities are highly prejudicial to its stated ideals when performed as professional functions. You simply cannot act in an authoritative role customarily and still remain dominantly professional, because being professional is not primarily a matter of technique but of supplying needed skills and strength in a spirit of service and dedication. The centurion who was accustomed to control men by the force of his commands properly proclaimed that he was unworthy that Christ should enter under his roof!

Thus the professional job still remains, regardless of the responsibilities individual members of the profession have had perforce to assume because our institutions are not equipped to supply the functions otherwise. Social work may take comfort in the fact that professional relationships can actually control the operation of administrative rules. A striking illustration of this is the well-known reduction-in-force technique in which "areas of competition" are defined. Employees within these defined areas are protected against claims of seniority or other preferential status held by those who do not function within the defined area. Existing professional relationships are a powerful force in defining these areas of competition. In plain language, the client tries to see that his professional adviser does not lose his job in the agency by which they both are employed because of another individual's right of seniority or veteran's preference. This, at least, is true of lawyers.

Another consideration in this issue is the troublesome question of loyalties. Privileged and confidential communication between professional and client in the course of their relationship, which is the very hallmark of a profession, is the chief means by which the professional is able to maintain his loyalty to his client. The subject has been dealt with by the author elsewhere in more technical terms.[1] To the extent that the professional is able to maintain silence with respect to disclosed personal facts and confidences, the professional ethic has again proved its strength. It is significant that all those safeguards by which the law surrounds and favors professional intimacy and confidential relationships have been applied successfully to relationships between the individual and a public agency.

Privileged communication is a legal concept. It means that the communications of the client to his professional adviser in

1. See "Reintegrating our Concepts of Privileged Communication," *Social Service Review*, June, 1942.

matters material to the purposes for which the professional relationship has been entered into, are protected in the sense that the adviser cannot, without violating his pledge as a member of his profession, disclose these communications to anyone *without his client's consent.* The test of the professional claim comes when such disclosure is sought to be avoided, at the wish of the client, in court or in some judicial proceeding. A statutory provision which purports to protect such communications, otherwise than in a court of law or in response to legal process, makes little sense, because if confidences are not protected in legal proceedings they are really not protected at all. You can compel disclosure. You sometimes see, for example, statutory provisions which say that such and such a statement or record shall not be disclosed except in response to a court order or subpoena. So you get a court order. It is not the function of a court to decide whether it would be more desirable to protect or disclose particular records. That is a legislative problem.

It is, therefore, of great value to the professional claim in social work that the privilege in the sense of the right to prevent or control disclosure of confidential information, exists in public as in private situations. The point is that the statute which authorizes agency regulations protective of such confidential information must in public offices act as a substitute for the conditions of the ordinary professional oath or pledge. The scope of the client's right to prevent disclosure is governed by the terms of the statute, and hence, of course, by the agency regulations issued thereunder.[2]

2. Regulation No. 1 of the Social Security Administration establishes a privilege in the claimant, although with sharply defined exceptions—such as the provisions authorizing release of certain information to a number of other state and federal agencies including those which administer public assistance and unemployment compensation. Other exceptions are in more general terms, such as that which forbids disclosure except "when consistent with efficient administration."

The contention that social work is not protected as a profession in this crucial area overlooks the fact that the agency through which the profession operates is usually authorized to issue regulations safeguarding confidential information.

The great distinction here is between confidential information pertinent to the professional services which are being accorded, and in respect of which the client can waive or refuse to waive his privilege, and agency-controlled facts, treated as state secrets, in which case the privilege belongs not to the client but to the agency or government to which it was communicated. The public interest in such cases is regarded as paramount and may result in withholding information which the client would be glad to release, or vice versa. The broad discretion claimed by some public agencies to maintain an independent control over the disposition of ordinary personal information, and to disclose or refuse to disclose personal items in its discretion, is one more symbol today of the substitution of administrative for legal controls.[3] It is rather obviously protective and paternalistic.

It is probable that legislative and judicial attitudes, which often exhibit hostility toward restrictions upon the use of personal information from the files of welfare departments particularly, are related to the general attitudes which regard welfare clients as social "dependents" and fail to recognize the ethical foundations of the client's right to economic security. The social dependent must conform.

But this brings us back again to the police power issue. This

3. The reader will not fail, however, to note the broad distinction between privileged communication of confidential information and the "secrecy" which may attach to lists of public assistance recipients. The latter provision is intended to conceal the identity of the communicant and hence establishes a "right of privacy" as distinguished from a legal privilege in respect of his communications to the agency. The demand for privacy may disappear as the function of public assistance becomes better understood and better integrated with other legal rights and objectives.

may be regarded as the larger threat to the standing of social work as a profession. Take, for example, the amendment in 1950 of Title IV of the Social Security Act [4] and the ensuing crop of statutes requiring workers in the Social Security program, as a condition to the award of assistance, to report to law enforcement officers the facts regarding the desertion of any individual child or mother. It must be obvious that just as long as we are at the call of those who would summon the police power to solve the same problem we are trying to solve by socio-economic programs and professional methods, we are apt to be called upon momentarily to betray a trust. This may occur whenever the police power steps in. Obviously, the professional method cannot be made to serve the police power without risking an utter betrayal of confidence and hence an utter perversion of ethical principles. The professional method invites confidences of the most intimate kind. A mother, for example, discloses to the social worker that her children are employed in occupations forbidden by law to those under a given age. Whenever a confidence thus invited and reposed for the purpose of enabling the professional person to see her problem and her situation as she herself sees it and to help her overcome it, is used as a means of establishing facts for judicial proceedings or for any police power purpose—perhaps for removing her children from the home, or to aid the legal prosecution of her husband, or of those with whom she has dealt, or for any purpose other than to obtain effective professional help in solving her own problems, the professional thesis has suffered an irremediable blow. It is like using a silken veil to remove grease.

The professional thesis is, of course, utterly vitiated by the common practice of using the purse strings of economic security to police society. Our daily bread becomes a baited

4. Social Security Act, § 402 (a) 10 as amended.

hook and is used as a behavior control. Beginning with the superficially harmless thesis that all that is intended is the maintenance of certain basic standards of living, it mushrooms into a device for inducing moral conformity and turns up ultimately as a device for political regimentation. An elderly woman, receiving old-age assistance, for example, was anonymously accused of spending money for betting at a race track. Her grant was stopped and she requested a hearing. The state director upheld the action discontinuing her grant because, in his view, even being seen at a race track was inappropriate for a recipient of assistance.

We must somehow keep our social processes from neutralizing or handicapping one another. We must keep the professional relationship utterly free of the charge that it has served an alien purpose. I am always troubled by a judicial decision holding that a juvenile court or a county court in a hearing on the question of the suitability of the child's parental guardianship, or on the question of his delinquency, should have access to all pertinent records of the welfare department, and even to the testimony of a professional social worker who has aided the child's mother or relatives in a professional capacity. Such decisions proceed on the bland assumption that the court is motivated only by a concern for the child and not to protect an interest which conflicts with those of the professional relationship it is thus abusing. The failure to protect confidential relationships kills the goose that lays the golden egg of ultimate understanding. You cannot in good faith ask a mother to open up to you voluntarily the secrets of her heart if you may be called upon to testify to this information in a proceeding brought to take the child from her custody. Is it consistent to compel such testimony and then condemn the one who gives it as a "snooper"?

A professional worker, for example, who may have been working with such a past parent or guardian in the effort to help him realize and carry out his responsibilities should not be called upon to testify in support of those who attack that guardian's fitness. The members of the profession who testify in the latter types of proceeding should not be forced or permitted to betray what has been communicated to them with the understanding that they will use it in support of the relationship under attack. When two partners decide to sever their relations, they require separate legal counsel. This elemental principle of professional loyalty is as applicable to one set of human relationships as it is to another.

The social worker will attain full professional status and recognition only when he is capable of "maintaining his loyalty" to his client's cause and can successfully and firmly reject any role or function which will compel the espousal of any purpose in conflict with his client's interest. No relationship can be effective as long as one of the parties to it is motivated by the need to protect independent interests with which the other party does not sympathize. This proves conclusively that the attainment of professional status is dependent upon the recognition of the right of the interests which the profession subserves to legal protection.

If a social worker, who has been guide and counsellor to a family or any of its members, is called to the police court or even the juvenile court in a delinquency proceeding, she cannot, as we have seen, then change her role and become a tool of the enforcement process without committing treason to her previous relationships with the family. The client remains her client and she remains in her individual professional relationship with that child or mother or father or family. The relationship cannot ethically be converted into an instrumentality for enforcing some law and certainly not when the enforcement proceeding has been undertaken in the belief, right or wrong, that the original professional undertaking has failed or is to be disavowed. The recognition of society's interest and concern does not lessen the need to observe ethical principles in the methods that are used.

Insist, if you must, that the interests of the individual and family should be harmonized with those of society and that the social worker is trying her best to do this; the fact remains that society and the individual often think each other wrong and both must be protected in the right to contend for their own point of view. The effort to adjust individual and social ends through pressure upon the individual or through compulsive means involves the judicial process, just as does the effort to enforce the rights of the individual. However, the judicial process was devised to protect the expression of opposite points of view and to arbitrate these differences. The judicial is a distinct function, a major function of government. The social agency is least of all a court; and a social worker is not a court or judge. Here is the ultimate test of the separateness of the professional and authoritative roles. The judicial function is, of course, authoritative. A social worker who confuses a court with a social agency betrays a fatal ignorance. Worse still, he does injury to his professional claim, for the tendency of social work to rely on administrative rather than legal techniques is most damaging to the professional claim.

Government should be required to observe the rules of professional ethics as faithfully as any other instrumentality. Its functions should be sufficiently differentiated to avoid embarrassment to its professional personnel. There is no use to deny that force and authority are necessary where the issue cannot be raised above the plane of force and authority. But if government is to serve individuals, it must seek to do so by the most efficacious methods and at the highest levels to which it can raise the issue. Hence professional relationships between the representatives of government and individuals should be eagerly encouraged. This assumes and requires that their con-

184

fidences be shielded and held sacred to the cause of human betterment for which they were undertaken.

This brings me to a brief consideration of functional compatibility in the profession of social work and departments of public welfare in this country, and in their relations with lawyers, courts, and judges.

Welfare agencies throughout the country are momentarily at the crossroads. We are so young, comparatively speaking, in our organized approach to social problems that we have not yet succeeded in achieving a scientific differentiation of function. The effort to unite many old boards and commissions in agencies charged with the administration of modern social legislation on a professional footing has resulted in great inconsistency of duties and loyalties. Welfare agencies have assumed a very broad responsibility for the administration of social legislation. They are expected to furnish professional service to children, to parents, to courts, and to many different agencies. They are charged with the administration of economic security laws, while they service police courts, juvenile courts, and courts of domestic relations. While helping mothers to rear their children, or even to adopt children, they are expected to furnish facts to district attorneys who prosecute husbands and putative fathers, who bring support actions, and who prosecute for abandonment. They are on all sides of the fence. I should say they are on both sides of the fence, servicing and policing. Yet the one inexorable condition to the success of professional work and professional relationships is the maintenance of loyalty to the cause of a client.

There seems to me to be but one answer to this conundrum. Welfare agencies must be freed of all police power responsibilities. The professional and the authoritative must be left to function independently of each other. Is it not obvious that the real threat to the cause of professionalism today is the inconsistency of function in the agencies which employ social workers?

You cannot exercise authoritative functions and professional functions at the same time, for either you will remain loyal to the one and disavow the other or you will serve the one and betray the other. The real question is whether the members of a profession can act professionally, serve their professional ends, and avoid violation of the professional pledge when they themselves are the means through which force and compulsion are brought to bear upon the individual whom they profess to serve in a professional capacity. The point is that functions should be performed by agencies properly constituted to perform them.

There are today three very different areas of function in many or most existing state welfare departments—entirely apart from those concerned merely with managing and supervising institutions. To begin with, most state welfare agencies are administering economic benefit laws or public assistance. Secondly, the agencies have assumed a very general responsibility for welfare services, the need for which is not necessarily related to the economic condition of the individual or family.

It is in the latter field that the profession of social work has found its most fruitful and typically professional undertakings. Almost any run-of-the-mill problem of living, by individual or family, may with great advantage use the skills and familiarity with social resources commanded by the modern professional social worker. In the field of children, especially, the agencies have a very considerable responsibility for establishing new human relationships and life opportunities. This typifies the contribution of this great new profession of social work to human freedom through the avenues of personal and interpersonal adjustment.

The Professional Idea

The rehabilitative process, in the broad sense which includes behavior and delinquency problems, with special emphasis on children, is the third field. Rehabilitation, as a current federal-state enterprise, is a mixture of physical restoration, training, and vocational guidance functions. The amendments passed in 1943 included mental cases insofar as they yield to medical treatment. Our conception of the rehabilitative process can thus easily be extended to include the treatment of most abnormal or unsocial behavior patterns, and in the adult group would be presently so conceived insofar as abnormal attitudes may affect earning power. These behavior patterns are gradually yielding in many instances to professional diagnosis and treatment. But partly through our ignorance, partly through the necessity of protecting the other fellow, and partly, no doubt, through the persistence of our more primitive resentments, the diagnosis and treatment have to be carried on under fairly rigid, authoritative controls, and are subject at all times to the intervention of the police power. In their professional aspects, they invoke specialized medical and psychiatric skills; and in their public-interest aspects they require judicial procedure capable of reconciling the aim of protecting society with the freedom and scope and independence that every professional person needs, if the professional approach is to have a real chance of success.

But it is not working in an authoritative setting that prejudices professionalism. Rather it is the *exercise of authority.* As we have seen, the professional, be he lawyer, social worker, or educator, serves many who are subject to rigid schemes of right and obligation. It is a fact that helping to secure the legal rights of those who most surely possess such rights, affords the best guarantee that the bounds of professionalism will not be overstepped. It is being authoritative, not serving those in authority, that raises questions of compatibility with professional attitudes.

187

Thus it is that preoccupation with child welfare, so-called, more than anything else, has raised questions about the nature of social work; for infants are in fact and indeed by definition incapable of decision. They are, as we have seen, "irresponsible." The social worker who works directly with a child as his alleged adviser must in some degree act as guardian and not as counsellor. However, the role of guardian is cautiously approached by workers and generally subsumed only in part. Even probation officers, aware of the conflict, attempt to maintain a certain balance between professional and authoritative functions.

The mere fact that one needs the scientific knowledge about people and about treatment that is part of the lore of social work, in order to perform one's duties in and about a welfare department or court, is obviously no evidence that the function to be performed is professional. Conversely, one can serve in a purely professional capacity in an institution that performs authoritative functions. It is not the setting. It is what you do and the circumstances under which you do it. Knowledge of law, for example, is a great aid to people in many different walks of life and in various positions of responsibility. This knowledge has no power in itself to determine the way in which it will be applied. Using one's knowledge of law in making decisions or in construing one's responsibilities is very different from using it as an advocate to solve a client's legal problem. Professional activity is recognized as a method of promoting a client's objectives through skills applied in the course of professional relationships.

Individual rights to medical services, on the basis of need for them, have not been established as yet. When they are, and when the body and mind are dealt with as a functioning unit, this teaming-up process on a functional basis will appropriately remove a large area of the behavior and delinquency problem from the ordinary welfare agency. The health function will be proportionately expanded. Then when economic problems are dealt with as economic problems and are separated from professional social service, the welfare agencies will be in a position to protect their distinct professional status, and to demonstrate their ability to do a really preventive and constructive job in the field of human relationships, which is the social work field par excellence.

But let us never forget the most fundamental of all functional differentiations, that between the legislative, executive, and judicial. Our first effort, therefore, should be to see that the legislature takes responsibility for defining human rights and duties of individuals and agencies in such form that the courts can deal with them. The legislature has followed, historically and too consistently, the practice of delegating the conscience of society, and with it a large measure of its lawmaking functions, first to single officials and more recently to public agencies. The function of defining rights and duties should not be delegated.

Fortified by a clear legislative statement of the individual's rights and of its own responsibilities, and appropriately limited in its functional concerns, the welfare agency would be in a position to service the courts in appropriate areas or to seek judicial action without prostituting its professional relationships, as well as to service existing personnel and family relationships. The agency, relieved of any obligation to serve the police power jurisdiction, will be able to work with the courts *in the creation of new relationships,* even though this properly involves in large measure the eliciting and proof of facts, for it will not be violating a trust in establishing and testifying to the facts for such purposes. It will be governed by no interests in conflict with its client's interest. Its client or clients in this picture are the parties to the prospective new relationship, be it guardianship, adoption, or some other relationship.

Concretely, the sound development I envisage here is the use by the court (guardianship, juvenile, or whatever it may be), of the personnel of the welfare agencies in the establishment of the physical facts—and also as experts in the establishment of the working principles—requisite to the creation by the court of human relationships by operation of law, be they guardianship, temporary or permanent, or adoption cases. Statutory provisions may or may not be essential to govern this function. In the main the service would be performed by professional personnel as witnesses, subject to cross-examination, after they have qualified themselves in the individual case. This is perhaps the best illustration that can be cited to orient us as to the correct relationships between agency and court.

The service agencies of society should remain pure service agencies, and no service should be undertaken as a public function except under circumstances in which it can be performed throughout on a wholly professional and non-authoritative basis. There is no better guide to sound social policy than this. Professional and authoritative attitudes are mutually antagonistic. When an attempt is made to combine them, they foul one another. Hence social agencies must eschew every authoritative role and resist every influence that prevents their action on a purely professional basis. This is true regardless of the age or capacity of the group with which they deal.

THE PROFESSION OF SOCIAL WORK

The professional idea, introduced into our governmental processes largely through the highly ethical doctrines and standards of the profession of social work, will ultimately, I think, become, if it is not so already, one of the strongest forces in maintaining individual freedoms, and hence in maintaining a really free society.

Let me recall at this point some things that seem to me

190

among the most significant, if less publicized, functions of the social work profession in our democracy. At the head of this list is the matter of individual freedom. I do not believe that regimentation is as great a menace to freedom as is the intricacy and complexity of the existing social order—a complexity that is increased, rather than lessened, by the very devices and mechanisms that we are developing to help the individual adjust himself. Freedom of choice in a labyrinth is of course a boomerang. There is no real power of decision without an adequate knowledge of alternatives and where they lead. Democracy itself is predicated upon the existence and expression of individual choice. If we are to preserve the basis for any kind of individual choice, indeed if we are to proceed as we are trying to do through the individual, there must exist an interpretative medium through which social scientists and members of the social work profession may succeed in reaching the individual more effectively than the commercial and political world can reach him, if not so expeditiously. That is the first concern.

The second function derives from the fact that our lawmakers, and our technical agencies and institutions as well, require extensive knowledge not only of the needs of human beings, but also of how they react to modern social laws and to various administrative methods. This is quite as important to the individual as is an understanding of the laws of society. This knowledge can come only from a comparative study and lively analysis of actual case histories by which we may derive a more adequate knowledge of human beings and their motivation. At the present time our law-makers and many of our social institutions are the victims of preconceptions that have the sanctity of tradition but not of scientifically reported experience. The social work profession provides us today with our most reliable social diagnoses.

In the third place, modern social science needs interpretation. Of course it needs more than interpretation. It needs application to life. This latter is, however, the core of any profession. What a profession does is to bring scientific knowledge to bear on the lives of people and to apply specialized skills and techniques to the resolution of their problems. But I am speaking at the moment of some important related functions of the profession. Our modern specialized skills and disciplines have been pursued by experts through many different channels and under the tutelage of many different organizations. These experts speak a language of their own. They need an interpreter, and not alone an interpreter, but an organization capable of harmonizing their various voices and orchestrating them into some kind of symphony.

A babel is always confusing, but a babel of experts is most confusing. It is obviously necessary not only that the agencies and instrumentalities of society but the experts that speak through these agencies shall reach the individual in unison. Is there not, then, a justification for a profession which is routinely conversant with many different aspects of social science, fluent in many tongues, and acquainted with the uses of many different institutions, to act as interpreter and coordinator of experts? This of course requires the ability to reduce their knowledge and their conclusions to simple terms for the purposes of synthesis and interpretation to the people who need them.

Fourthly, legislation is directing itself to the creation of new rights of a personal nature. It is indeed high time that we concern ourselves with the creation of a system of human rights, which, if not as well systematized as our older property law, may at least help us to realize the legal ideal of a system of laws built around the individual. Personal rights need for their effective realization the services of a professional like that of social work, for personal rights do not lend themselves, in the same degree, to the scientific precisions of property law. Ideal interpretation of them is vital if they are to prevail. Introducing the spirit of reason, sound thinking, and the strength that comes from knowledge of one's right, is essential if the laws establishing personal rights are not to be prejudiced in their operation. Securing the active cooperation of the individual is a condition precedent to their effective administration.

Finally, there is need for an organization to consolidate our social gains and carry them into the future. Political systems may come and go, but whatever we have succeeded in adding to life and to the enrichment of life must carry on. A profession once organized is one of the most permanent of human institutions. It is a highway to the future.

Chapter 13

FREEDOM AND RESPONSIBILITY

T HE TEST OF freedom is adjustment, not caprice. A mechanism that is precise and well-adjusted in terms both of its own individual parts and of its relations with other mechanisms outside itself, is free. Capricious and unrelated action creates confusion. By destroying the freedom of others, it destroys ultimately all freedom of its own. You get a new vehicle of transportation and drive it on a modern highway. The machinery is precision-made. The different vehicles and movements along the way are given independence in proportion as highway engineering has provided a more scientific framework of the road. The motor hums and you begin to catch a sense of mastery and freedom. And if you yourself are properly adjusted to this basic framework, your growing sense of freedom is not the least impeded by the fact that you cannot jump the track and indulge in an utterly erratic mode of driving.

In the same way individuals in society can move independently within the legal framework of the road and achieve the same sense of freedom. The framework of the road along which we proceed is provided by the system of legal rights and obligations that control our relations with one another.

194

This system or framework is objective and circumstantial, and, when well constructed, makes us independent of personal supervision. General observance of the rules makes it unnecessary for the will of the policeman to intervene.

Human beings and human relationships, delicate, sensitive, and finely processed as they are, are capable of an infinitely fine, precise, frictionless, and efficient adjustment. This is true both inwardly and outwardly, both subjectively and objectively. Therefore, individuals can achieve a sense of perfect freedom in a society that is legally well engineered. The achievement of this sense of freedom lessens the inclination to jump the track and drive capriciously; for the desire of the individual to be free is satisfied by the easy adjustments provided for by the framework of the road and his resulting ability to achieve his aims without interference.

If this be true, it follows at once that the human ideal is not to be realized in the power to crash willy-nilly through opposing odds in utter self-reliance, but rather in achieving an ethic in human relationships that will make for the best adjustment and the greatest individual freedom. But if we refuse to create human rights and to safeguard the equal prerogatives and self-expression of the weaker elements in our society, we but promote a system in which one individual is forced to seek his ends by attaching himself as a parasite to the back of another. You have seen this happen countless times upon the highway when, in a general mix-up, one car making a pathway for itself, others follow, losing for the time being all independence of movement, and ruthlessly cutting off all other movements. It is a game of following the leader but not of obedience to law. Human society can easily reach a similar impasse.

We attach a great value to self-reliance. Analyze this matter of self-reliance. You find that it is a matter of exploiting your environment. By exploiting, I mean drawing upon or making use of whatever lies around you that you can use to maintain and develop your life. This is a legitimate process. But, as we have seen, our environment is now, in the main, our fellow men. What do you do with this elemental fact? I see life exploiting nature as its prerogative, its right, if you please. I see the individual doing the same thing in society to the extent that he has rights in the society we have created. As life seeks adjustment to its physical environment, from which it draws the needs of its life, so men do in society. But the ethical system that gives life its freedom and prerogative, in this respect derives its value from the fact that it effectively adjusts human relationships, and so enables men freely to attain their ends.

You cannot, therefore, promote freedom, or express your freedom, by advancing yourself at the expense of others, and so throwing your relationships into imbalance. You must advance your relationship with others. You must work within the framework of the road.

The idea that freedom will ever exist in the absence of law or in realms beyond law denies the most fundamental principle in all creation. Freedom, perfect freedom, will always co-exist with and be founded upon a declared ethic by which the human will, of its own volition, will be guided and which it will by its acts maintain and effectuate. The rights of man and the duties of man will continue to be expressed, albeit with a growing precision and refinement. What man does or wills to do will yet be voluntary and ever be regarded as such, for he will find in law the means of achieving his objectives. The obviously efficient and effective road to his determined ends will be within the framework of the codes of his own devising.

But this means that the individual will have assumed full responsibility for his acts and for the consequences of his acts. The human race can be assured of freedom in a legally ruled society in proportion to the sharpness of its sense of responsibility as individuals. Freedom and responsibility are correlatives. They are the opposite sides of the legal coin.

It is significant that the law's concern for maintaining freedom varies inversely with its need to be concerned about maintaining responsibility in any given situation. This shifting emphasis is perhaps best illustrated by our attitudes in relation to the use of the insurance principle, for by insurance we transfer the burden of loss from the individual to a group, or even to society at large.

Consider, first, situations in which deliberate action is involved. Here our concern with the individual's sense of responsibility is paramount. Society might, for example, decide to underwrite the losses arising from the unsocial behavior of juveniles. This would serve a useful purpose in spreading the burden of losses so caused, for they are highly erratic and unpredictable in their incidence, but one would hardly propose such a scheme, insofar as it might tend to lessen the sense of individual responsibility. At least this would be a paramount consideration wherever the individual was old enough to be charged with any sense of responsibility.

At the opposite end of the scale one can cite the example of workmen's compensation. Here our concern about responsibility is at a minimum since it is not possible to say with certainty what effect the pooling of funds and the imposition of liability without proof of negligence has upon the assumption of responsibility for safe conditions and the conduct of fellow workmen. However, legal science found it difficult to uphold this reform under the Constitution insofar as it deprived the individual of his freedom of contract. In fact, it was considered necessary to show that this freedom of contract was more illusory than real under the circumstances, and that the need for protection through resort to the police power was paramount.

In between these two extremes we might cite the highway

accident situation. Here we find ourselves in the realms of pure negligence, including lack of skill and foresight. No contractual relationships are involved. It is held that individuals may be required to take out liability insurance, a fact that is in some degree a deprivation of freedom. On the other hand, through the insurance principle the individual is relieved of responsibility for loss. His liability is thus confined to paying the insurance premium. It is interesting to consider to what extent the individual's sense of responsibility for the total result, that is to say, for the maintenance of high standards on the highway, and hence for low premium rates, is maintained despite this shift of responsibility from the individual to the group of which he is a member.

I confess to a feeling that my life's record should always be regarded as pertinent wherever it can be deemed relevant. I have a feeling, for example, that my personal driving record should constitute a factor in measuring the extent of my highway insurance obligation. I feel, however, that this is a true corollary to my conviction that we should pool our resources and capacities to the extent necessary to meet our needs and that we can do so under existing conditions without prejudice to the sense of personal responsibility for the important issues of life.

I think that there has been developing, along with social and economic conditions, an awareness on the part of individual members of society that their personal responsibility is not lessened by the shifting of the burden from the person himself to a pooled fund to which he contributes, and that we can therefore adopt in this way far more effective measures to maintain health and security and to develop educational and other constructive programs to better our human environment. At the opposite extreme of political thought there stand those who would provide medical care, for example, only where personal fault or blame could not be assigned for the injury or illness from which the individual suffered. While it may be that our faith in the maintenance of the individual's sense of responsibility in a social complex may be dependent in part upon the changed conditions of life, I think that our conviction about it must also be influenced by the knowledge that we are gaining as to the real goals and incentives of life. The social instinct of individuals is strong, and the sense of responsibility, on which we rely, was gained, throughout the entire history of man's development, in an environment adamantly ruled by law.

I see no reason why society should not be bound to the full extent that it can effectively serve the life of the individual. In so doing, we give the individual the maximum of freedom. We make each individual an *heir to the combined power of our varied capacities*. We give him a really responsive environment. We make society the servant of man as nature is the servant of life. It should be.

The great mistake of the human race is to set on high the product of its own hands, and then to fall down and worship it. "Thou shalt not make unto thee any graven image.... Thou shalt not bow down to them nor worship them." The society we create should by virtue of the laws that govern it, become the servant of human life. Our society should be made to serve us. That purpose it will best fulfil to the extent that it undertakes to meet need wherever it finds it.

There is a profound and unmistakable cleavage between the processes of giving and taking, between the dedication of our human capacities and the servicing of our human needs. As we have seen, our basic needs are common to us all. Our individual capacities are never quite comparable.

I am greatly troubled to hear the word "socialism" applied to the use of the instrumentalities and agencies of organized society to assure the meeting of our needs. We are speaking here only of the distributive process. Governmental agencies which enter directly into the productive function involve themselves in the exercise of authority, whereas the mere introduction of a need factor into our distributive process and the interposition of controls in that process essential to see that basic needs of individuals are met, can be achieved without the exercise of productive management or direct participation in industrial enterprise. Moreover, I am influenced in my dislike of authoritative methods by the fact that the interposition of these controls and the use of the tax power for this purpose can be highly effective when used in substitution for such dictatorial methods as price-fixing and other restraints upon human initiative. The same philosophy which would deny the desirability of government's taking over the products of industry and making distributions of these products in kind, would likewise dictate the wisdom of refraining from controlling or directing the productive capacities of the individual.

We must of course avoid forcing the varied faculties of mankind into a single mold in our concentration on specific methods. We need nature's freedom in her exploration of the infinite to find better and better answers to the problems that nature encounters. A government which did not find itself responsive to the demands for standardization and the confinement of its activities to the pursuit of a proved method would be an unresponsive government. It seems to me, however, that governmental agencies can be used to insure better distribution without curtailing initiative in devising new methods, new techniques, and new products. It can, through the tax power, create the right to a basic income while in no way conditioning its use. It can provide insurance against genuine hazards. It can contract for the construction of needed facilities for purposes that meet common needs such as roads, hospitals, schools, rehabilitation centers, clinics, libraries, and other standardized and universally needed facilities. Moreover, in the case of those enterprises that are undertaken to supply individuals with genuinely professional services, it can proceed by purchase or employment of such services. In this area it can safely operate. It can employ professional skills for professional servicing on a free and non-authoritative basis in respect both of the client and the skill employed. It can place its faith in standards of professional qualification and so undertake the servicing of individuals on a professional basis. It can service the created rights of the individual.

In the case of all these activities, it can supply what is fundamentally standardized while providing for the development of what is not standardized and encouraging progressive and experimental activity. The great difference here is between engaging in commercial activities, in the production, as well as in the purchase and sale of commodities, on the one hand, and on the other hand, serving the individual, making facilities available to him, and seeing to it that he is able to use them.

Today individual need is not met, or is met on a selective basis in violation of the equal-protection-of-the-law principle. This results in a demand that government be placed in charge of productive enterprise. This is common experience everywhere. It reflects, however, the substitution of personal direction and supervision for the system of law and legal rights and obligations that alone permits society to function autonomously. It is plainly recidivistic in all its implications. That is the situation we have to meet today.

In general, government can effectively serve the individual, but cannot effectively manage him. For all of these reasons, resort to the tax process in gradual substitution for the police power and in preference to taking over and assuming responsibility for the management of productive processes, seems to me the way toward freedom; provided, of course, the taxes are paid in relation to capacity. The tax process concentrates upon property rather than upon persons. You can take property without taking the individual or his freedom; yet in the economic sphere it is a control of very general efficacy. Social security rests squarely upon it as does our hope for a reasonably well balanced economy. It has seemed to me more and more the test of the survival of our society.

The summation of it all is the fact that society is our creation. Our job is to continue to work positively in its construction. We need above all else to call upon our imaginations in this creative process. One of our greatest difficulties is the fact that everything that we achieve fills us with a dread fear that we may lose it. The preservation of what we have engrosses our activities. It would not be so if we were working continually to make things better instead of trying merely to preserve what we have. We need to see, for example, the great promise for the future that exists in a more ethically motivated social order. We need to see the advantage that would accrue to all of us if every individual about us had the means of realizing more of his potential capacity.

Imagination, especially in his approach to the individual, is the most important asset of a social scientist. The gross deception that inheres in appearances is, I suppose, one of the greatest challenges to the mind of man. The truth is that the one thing that we can be really sure of is that neither people nor things are actually what they outwardly appear to be. It is this fact more than anything else that should stimulate our curiosity and drive us on.

Take, for example, that exposition of John C. Bennett in his *Christian Ethics and Social Policy*. He shows effectively how Christ tore to shreds most of our preconceived ideas about social values. Christ substituted his plus signs for our minus signs, and minus signs for our plus signs. In this way he dealt "with the respectable and the outcast, with the righteous and the sinners, with the rich and the poor, with the diplomatic order and the subservient washing of the client's feet, with the Samaritan and the priest and Levite, with the prodigal son and the elder brother, with the lords of the earth and those who serve, with the ninety and nine and the one...." [1]

We must then give our imagination and our faith full rein in any analysis that we may seek to make about the reactions of human beings to the transformations that we may bring about in our human society. This indeed we must do if we would create, yes, even a garden. In this vein I planted a shrub here and another there. Seeking to combine different ideas, I built a fountain but I depressed my fountain below the surface of the earth so that the flowers might furnish the rim of the fountain and the fountain might water the flowers. In the same vein, I began to build a little building, low set, and of hard cement. A child entered this building and asked me what it was and I asked her what it looked like and she said, "Well, it could be a Church or a Sunday School, for it has an Altar and a Cross and some colored glass, and a bell; but then it also has growing things inside and outside and a glass roof and water and a place for flowers. What is it, anyway?" And all I could say was that it was not finished, if indeed it ever will be finished, and it did not yet appear what it might be, but as it had earth and fire and air and water, and sound and color, and strength, and, as I hoped, beauty, and religion, then unless my imagination had played me false it should be possible from all these elements to compose something new and individualized. For, you see, I was playing here with different values, hoping in the process of their interrelationship to discover some fresh significance.

And then my mind ran to this whole confused world at the moment and its utterly irreconcilable currents and conflicts, and I began to think of what appeared to me to be some of

1. John C. Bennett, *Christian Ethics and Social Policy* (New York, Charles Scribner's Sons, 1946), p. 11.

the outward signs of very real significant new values in it. I thought of the scientist turned political realist, of the cartoonist who points an accusing finger at Uncle Sam, sternly asking whether he has actually become so communally minded as to join an international organization, of the psychiatrist who has literally reversed our notions of strength and weakness in human behavior, and finally of the scientist again who stands bewildered before the reversal of his own plus and minus signs, who finds one supposedly ultimate physical law after another denied or reversed, until at last the very altars of the conservative idea are overthrown. These effects appear only as the imagination has been given rein and as we have been given to deny the reality of the obvious and to substitute a truth that is the very reverse of the apparent.

The welfare enterprise has moved forward from its traditions as a differentiated branch of human endeavor and it has joined forces with other great currents of human tradition, with the psychological, economic, and now with the legal, and as a result of this confluence of ancient values, an entirely new mixture has been formed and it does not yet appear what it shall be; but it may be that our ultimate triumphs do spring from our imaginations. And the question is whether our imaginations play us false or whether we shall, with all these new factors, create something that is something, and of which we too can say, "It is good."

www.ingramcontent.com/pod-product-compliance
Lightning Source LLC
Chambersburg PA
CBHW020351270326
41926CB00007B/386